COTTON
KNITS

COTTON KNITS

Edited by Sally Harding

WINDWARD · FRANCES LINCOLN

CONTENTS

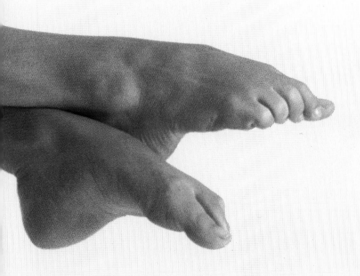

Cotton Knits
© Frances Lincoln Limited 1987
Reprinted 1987

Cotton Knits was conceived, edited and designed
by Frances Lincoln Limited, Apollo Works,
5 Charlton Kings Road, London NW5 2SB

WINDWARD
an imprint owned by W.H. Smith and Son Limited
Registered No. 237811, England
Trading as WHS Distributors
St. John's House, East Street, Leicester LE1 6NE

ISBN 0 7112 0457 8

Printed and bound in Hong Kong by
Kwong Fat Offset Printing Co. Ltd.
Filmsetting by Bookworm Typesetting, Manchester

COLOUR & COTTON

Cotton yarn is not uniformly graded in the same way that wool is. We have therefore divided the cotton yarns used by the designers in this book into four types. In the materials paragraph in the patterns, we specify fine, light and medium weights, and fancy yarns (bouclé, slub, chenille, towelling etc). Fine yarns are approximately the equivalent of 2-ply wool, lightweight of 4-ply and medium weight of double knitting wool. You will be able to match the correct yarn to the design with the help of the life-size length of yarn photographed on the same page as the garment, and by checking ball bands which usually recommend needle size and tension. You *must* knit a tension square to check the yarn before you embark on the pattern (see page 110), changing the needles, if necessary, to give the specified tension.

Some of the designs are knitted up using two strands of yarn throughout. Unless this is for the specific purpose of achieving subtle colour effects (see page 33) or texture (see page 98), you could replace two strands of fine yarn, say, with one of a lightweight yarn but, again, the only way to check if this will measure the same as the pattern is to work a tension square first.

The colour scheme is a crucial factor in the success of any knitted garment. Many knitters follow the designer's colour choice because it suits them or they lack the confidence to mix colours. To help you plan an alternative colour scheme, we have shown knitted alternative colourways to some of the designs in this book. It is possible to mix colours successfully and to make quite radical and attractive changes to the original design as a result.

There are some simple guidelines to help you towards a successful choice. Firstly, look at your main colour choice and hold up at least four balls of the yarn to get some idea of the strength of the colour when spread over a larger area. When you are mixing colours together, if the pattern is a large one, hold up a number of balls, but if it's a tiny pattern, hold strands of the yarn together to get a clearer idea of the final effect. Secondly, separate your choice of colours out into the basic groups – the soft pastels, the striking bright colours, the neutrals and the strong but subtle shades – photographed below. Mix any of the colours in these groups with white and you will be successful, but mixing the first and last groups, for example, takes more skill. Good designers often break the 'rules' with

great success (see Racing colours, page 50), but you need a good colour sense and a great deal of confidence in what looks good on you to succeed. If you are not sure of your choice, colour in blocks with crayon or pencil to see how the colours work together to help you visualize the final effect.

The fashion drawings on these pages show how a designer has done this using two of the designs in the book. Mondrian squares (see page 26), with its clear grid design, is easily worked in new colourways. On one of the drawings, texture has been emphasized by the stitch patterns using a single neutral tone or shades of neutral tones. The bright version shows how different brights have been mixed together on a neutral background.

Crazy paving (see page 88) is also designed around a frame of a single colour. If you want to make a big statement, reverse the colours in the knitted up sweater or fill in the frames with murky pastels or brights. The illustration on the left shows how similar tones – grey and pale yellow – take the boldness out of the design and give it a quiet, elegant sophistication. The sketched colour squares show how much the design alters by different combination.

The Mondrian squares design is a classic shape that looks good with any number of different colour combinations.

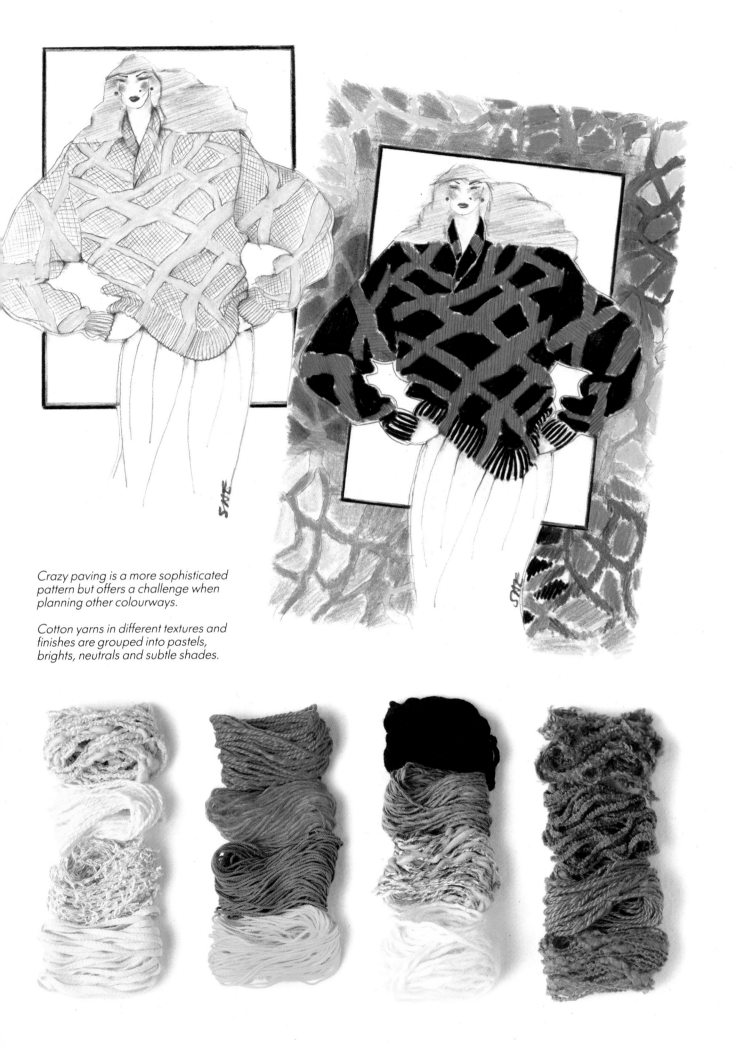

Crazy paving is a more sophisticated pattern but offers a challenge when planning other colourways.

Cotton yarns in different textures and finishes are grouped into pastels, brights, neutrals and subtle shades.

IN THE PINK

This plain-collared shirt can be knitted up with long or short sleeves. You can choose from two other cable patterns, shown on page 13, to alter the effect.

◼ SIZE
One size to fit up to 97cm/38in bust.
See diagram for finished measurements.

◼ MATERIALS
Use a medium weight cotton yarn.
800g for short sleeve version
900g for long sleeve version
One pair each of 4mm and 5mm knitting needles *or size to obtain correct tension*
One cable needle
Three 15mm buttons

◼ TENSION
22 sts and 24 rows to 10cm over st st using larger needles
Check your tension before beginning.

◼ BACK
Using smaller needles, cast on 95 sts and work in rib as foll:
1st rib row (RS) K1, *P1, K1, rep from * to end.
2nd rib row P1, *K1, P1, rep from * to end.
Rep last 2 rows until rib measures 3cm, ending with a first row.
Inc row Rib 1, (M1, rib 3) 14 times, (M1, rib 2) 4 times, (M1, rib 3) 14 times, M1, rib 2. 128 sts.
Change to larger needles and work in patt as foll:
1st row (RS) P7, *K2, P3, K8, P3, K2, P3, K8, P3, K2*, P46, rep from * to *, P7.
2nd row K7, *P2, K3, P8, K3, P2, K3, P8, K3, P2*, K46, rep from * to *, K7.
3rd to 6th rows As first and 2nd.
7th row P7, *K2, P3, slip next 4 sts onto cable needle and hold at back of work, K4 from LH needle, K4 from cable needle – called C8, P3, K2, P3, C8, P3, K2*, P46, rep from * to *, P7.
8th row As 2nd row.
These 8 rows form patt.
Cont in patt without shaping until back measures 61cm from beg, ending with a WS row.

Shoulder shaping
Cast off 11 sts at beg of next 8 rows.
Cast off rem 40 sts.

◼ FRONT
Work as for back until front measures 28cm from beg, ending with a RS row.
Divide for centre front opening.
Next row (WS) Work 61 sts in patt, P1, (K1, P1) 3 times. Turn and leave rem sts on a spare needle.

Next row K1, (P1, K1) 3 times, work in patt to end.
Rep last 2 rows until opening measures 3cm, ending with a WS row.
Work buttonhole as foll:
1st buttonhole row Rib 3, cast off 2, rib 2, work in patt to end.
2nd buttonhole row Work in patt to last 7 sts, rib 2, cast on 2, rib 3.
Cont in patt and work another 2 buttonholes at 8cm intervals.
Work 2 rows more in patt. (Front should now measure approx 48cm.)

Neck shaping
Next row With RS facing, cast off 16 sts, work in patt to end. 52 sts.
Work one row.
Keeping patt correct, dec one st at neck edge on next and every foll alternate row 7 times. 44 sts.
Work without shaping until front matches back to beg of shoulder shaping, ending with a RS row.

Shoulder shaping
Cast off 11 sts at beg of next and 2 foll alternate rows.
Work one row. Cast off rem 11 sts.
With WS facing, rejoin yarn to rem 60 sts, cast on 8 sts for button border. 68 sts.
Next row (WS) P1, (K1, P1) 3 times, work in patt to end.

Next row Work in patt to last 7 sts, K1, (P1, K1) 3 times.
Work to match first side, omitting buttonholes.

■ SLEEVES (Make 2)

**Using smaller needles, cast on 59 sts and work in rib as for back for 3cm, ending with a RS row.
Inc row Rib 1, (M1, rib 3) 8 times, (M1, rib 2) 4 times, (M1, rib 3) 8 times. M1, rib 2. 80 sts.**
Change to larger needles and work in patt as foll:
1st row (RS) K23, work from * to * as first row of back, P23.
2nd row P23, work from * to * as 2nd row of back, K23.
These 2 rows place centre cable panel. Shape sides by inc one st at each end of every 3rd row until there are 100 sts. Cont without shaping until sleeve measures 28cm from beg.
Cast off.

■ COLLAR

Join shoulder seams.
With RS facing and using smaller needles, beg in middle of right front band and pick up and K40 sts up right front neck, 35 sts across back neck and 40 sts down left front neck to centre of left front band. 115 sts.
Work in rib as for back for 10cm, beg with a 2nd row.
Cast off loosely in rib.

■ MAKING UP

Sew sleeve edge to front and back, placing centre of cable panel to shoulder seam.
Join side and sleeve seams.
Sew cast on edge of left front band underneath right front band.
Sew on buttons.
Press according to instructions on yarn label.

LONG SLEEVE VERSION

■ BACK AND FRONT

Work as for short sleeve version.

■ SLEEVES (Make 2)

Work as for short sleeve version from ** to **.
Change to larger needles and work in patt as for short sleeve version *and at the same time* shape sides by inc one st at each end of every 7th row until there are 100 sts.
Work without shaping until sleeve measures 44cm from beg. Cast off.

■ MAKING UP AND COLLAR

Work as for short sleeve version.

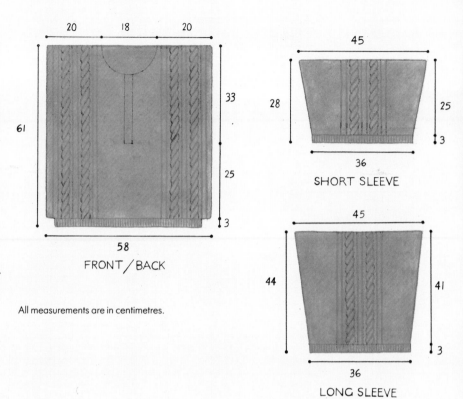

20   18   20

33

61   25

3

58

FRONT / BACK

All measurements are in centimetres.

45

28   25

3

36

SHORT SLEEVE

45

44   41

3

36

LONG SLEEVE

These four samples show the three cable stitches knitted up in alternative bright colourways.

CABLE VARIATIONS

You may like to ring the changes by knitting this classic shirt shape with a different cable pattern. Remember to check your tension before embarking on the new pattern. The two cables shown in the red and blue variations below can be incorporated into the master pattern by using the pattern below to replace the stitches which appear between the * and * in the main pattern.

■ RED CABLE

1st row K2, P3,(sl 2 sts onto cable needle, hold at back of work, K2, then K2 from cable needle – called CB4 –,) twice, P3, K2, P3, CB4 twice, P3, K2.
2nd row P2, K3, P8, K3, P2, K3, P8, K3, P2.

3rd row K2, P3, (sl 2 sts onto cable needle, hold at front of work, K2, then K2 from cable needle – called CF4 –,) twice, P3, K2, P3, CF4 twice, P3, K2.
4th row As 2nd row.
These 4 rows form patt.

■ BLUE CABLE

1st row K2, P4, K2, P2, K2,P4, K2, P4, K2, P2, K2, P2, K2, P4, K2.
2nd row P2, K4, P2, K2, P2, K4, P2, K4, P2, K2, P2, K2, P2, K4, P2.
3rd row K2, P4, sl next 4 sts onto cable needle and hold at front of work, K2, sl 2 purl sts from cable needle back onto LH needle, pass the cable needle to back of work, P2 from LH needle, K2 from cable needle – called MB4 –,P4, K2, P4, MB4, P4, K2.
4th row and every alternate row As 2nd row.
5th row and every alternate row As first row.
10th row As 2nd row.
These 10 rows form patt.

ORCHID SPRAY

This cardigan can be converted simply to a waistcoat by leaving off the sleeves and making armhole bands. For a simpler design, leave out the orchid motif. An alternative clematis motif is given overleaf.

■ SIZE

To fit 81-86[91-97-102]cm/32-34[36:38-40]in bust
Figures for larger sizes are given in square brackets. Where there is only one set of figures, this applies to all sizes.
See diagram for finished measurements.

■ MATERIALS

Use a fine cotton fleck yarn and a viscose yarn knitted together throughout for the main colour (A). Use a lightweight cotton yarn for contrast colours.
475[475:500]g main colour A viscose (silver)
275[300:325]g main colour A cotton (beige/pink fleck)
30g 1st contrast B (pink)
40g 2nd contrast C (green)
25g 3rd contrast D (yellow)
30g 4th contrast E (blue)
For waistcoat version:
325[325:350]g main colour A viscose
225[225:250]g main colour A cotton
One pair each of 4½mm and 5½mm knitting needles *or size to obtain correct tension*
One 2.50mm crochet hook
One pair shoulder pads
Two 35mm buttons
Three 20mm buttons

■ TENSION

16 sts and 20 rows to 10cm over st st using larger needle
Check your tension before beginning.

■ Note

Read chart from right to left for RS knit rows and left to right for WS purl rows. Unless stated st st is used throughout. Use separate balls of yarn for each area, do not carry yarn across back of work. Take care to twist yarns at the back when changing colours to avoid holes forming (see page 114).

■ BACK

Using smaller needles and A, cast on 83[89:95] sts and work in rib as foll:
1st rib row (RS) K1, *P1, K1, rep from * to end.
2nd rib row P1, *K1, P1, rep from * to end.
Rep last 2 rows until rib measures 3cm, ending with a 2nd rib row inc one st in last row. 84[90:96] sts.
Change to larger needles and work without shaping from row 1 of chart for back (outer line) to the end of row 62.

Armhole shaping

Cast off 6 sts at beg of next 2 rows.
Dec one st at each end of next and every alternate row 4 times in all. 64[70:76] sts.
Cont without shaping to the end of row 116.

Shoulder shaping

Cast off 5[6:7] sts at beg on next 4 rows.
Cast off 6[7:8] at beg of next 2 rows.
Cast off rem 32 sts.

■ RIGHT FRONT

Using larger needles and A, cast on 2 sts, and work from row 1 of chart for front as foll:
1st row Work in patt to end.
2nd row Inc one st at beg of row, work in patt to end.
3rd row Inc one st at each end of row.
4th row Cast on 3 sts at beg of row, work in patt to last st, inc one st. Rep last 2 rows 5 times. (14th row of chart) 39 sts.
Next row Inc one st at beg of row, work in patt to last 0[1:1] st, inc 0[1:1].
Next row Cast on 0[2:3] sts, work in patt to last st, inc one st.
Next row Inc one st at beg of row, work in patt to last 0[0:0] st, inc one st.
Next row Inc 0[0:1] st, work in patt to end. 42[45:48] sts.
Cont without shaping to the end of row 56 of chart.

Front shaping

Next row (RS) Dec one st at beg of row, work in patt to end.
Work in patt for 4 rows without shaping.
Rep last 5 rows to end of row 79 of chart. 37[40:43] sts.

Armhole shaping

Next row (WS) Cast off 4[5:6] sts, work in patt to end.
Work one row.
Cont to dec at front edge on every 5th row from previous *dec and at the same time* dec one st at armhole edge on next and every alternate row 3 times more. 27[29:31] sts.
Keeping armhole edge straight, cont to dec at front edge on every 5th row from previous dec to the end of row 133. 18:[20:22] sts.

Shoulder shaping

Cast off 5[6:7] sts at beg of next and 2 foll alternate rows.
Cast off rem 8 sts.

■ LEFT FRONT

Work as for right front, reversing all shapings and working a mirror image of chart by beg with a P row instead of a K row.

■ SLEEVES (Make 2)

Using smaller needles and A, cast on 43 sts and work in rib as for back for 3cm, ending with a WS row.
Inc row Rib 4, (M1, rib 3) 13 times. 56 sts.
Change to larger needles and work from sleeve chart (thicker line on back chart) as foll:

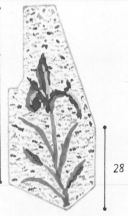

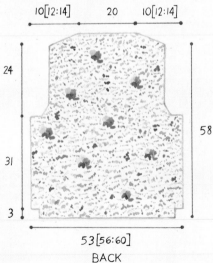

40

5

48

40

35

3

11 [13:14]

SLEEVE

10[12:14]   20   10[12:14]

24

31

3

58

53[56:60]

BACK

26 [28:30]

RIGHT FRONT

28

Inc one st at each end of 3rd and every foll 4th row to 84 sts.
Cont without shaping until the end of row 80.

Top of sleeve shaping
Cast off 6 sts at beg of next 2 rows.
Dec one st at each end of next and every foll alternate row 4 times in all. 64 sts.
Cast off.

■ BACK BELT
Using smaller needles and A, cast on 13 sts and work in K1, P1 rib for 20cm.
Cast off loosely in rib.

■ MAKING UP
**To finish pointed edges on fronts, crochet a chain st edging along pointed edges to give a straighter edge.
Work each side of point separately.
Sew in all ends and press pieces on back under damp cloth or with a steam iron**.
Join shoulder seams.
Sew top of sleeve to armhole edge.
Join sleeve and side seams.

■ FRONT BAND
With RS facing and using smaller needles and A, pick up and K109 sts evenly up right front edge to centre back neck and 110 sts down left front edge. 219 sts.
Work in P1, K1 rib for one row.
1st buttonhole row Rib 3, cast off 3, (rib 12, cast off 3) twice, rib 183.
2nd buttonhole row Rib 183, cast on 3, (rib 12, cast on 3) twice, rib 3.
Work 2 rows more in rib.
Cast off loosely in rib.
Sew smaller buttons to front band.
Attach belt by sewing one large button at each end, placing belt at waist level approx 10cm from lower edge at centre back of garment.

SLEEVELESS WAISTCOAT VERSION

■ BACK AND FRONTS
Work as for cardigan.

■ ARMHOLE BANDS
Join shoulder seams.
With RS facing and using smaller needles and A, pick up and K96 sts around armhole.
Work in K1, P1 rib for 3cm.
Cast off loosely in rib.

■ MAKING UP
Work as for cardigan version from ** to **.
Join side and armhole band seam.
Work front band and complete as for cardigan.

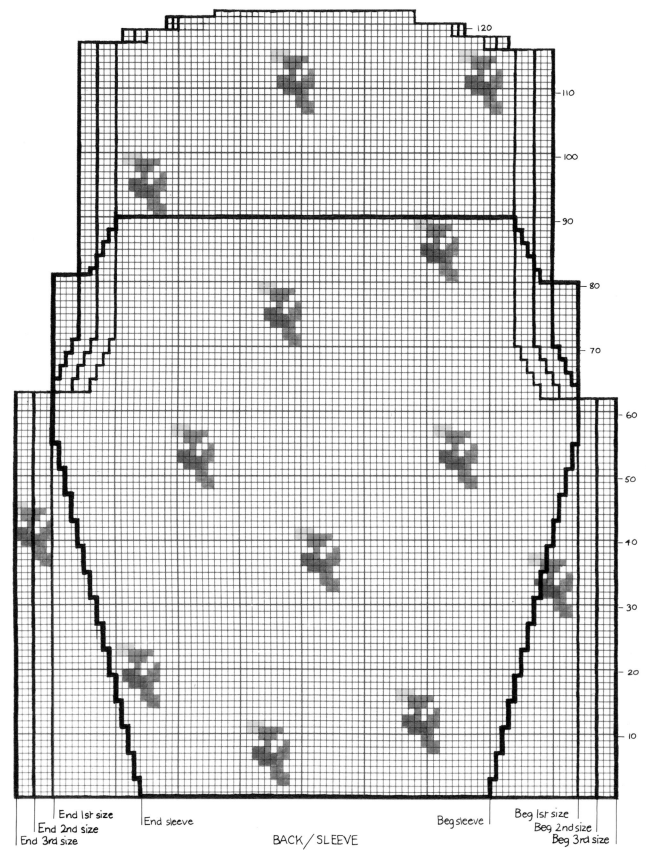

120

110

100

90

80

70

60

50

40

30

20

10

End 1st size

End 2nd size

End 3rd size

End sleeve

Beg sleeve

Beg 1st size

Beg 2nd size

Beg 3rd size

BACK / SLEEVE

16

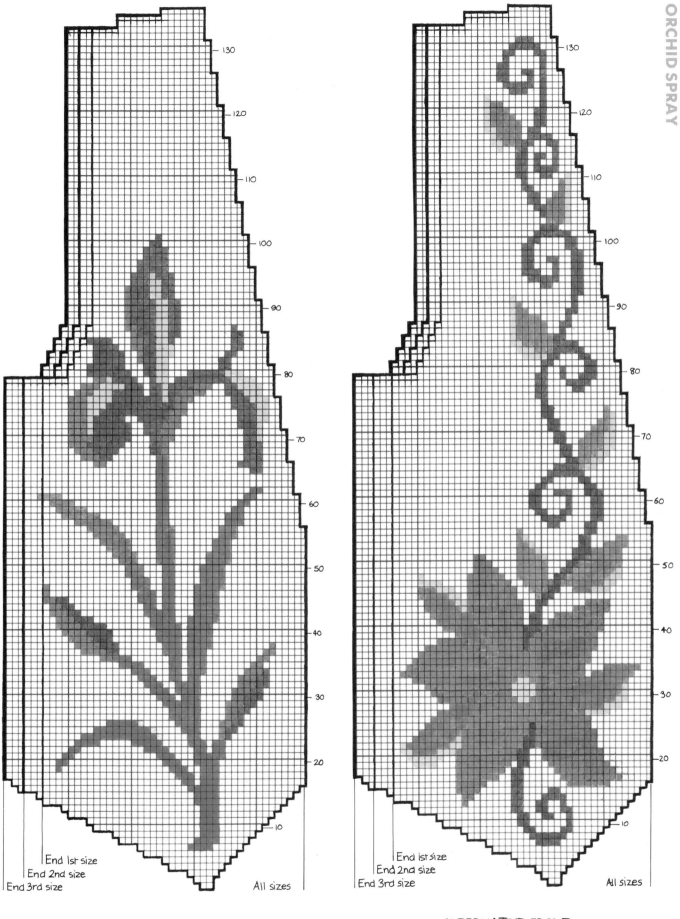

— 130
— 120
— 110
— 100
— 90
— 80
— 70
— 60
— 50
— 40
— 30
— 20
— 10

End 1st size
End 2nd size
End 3rd size
All sizes

RIGHT FRONT

— 130
— 120
— 110
— 100
— 90
— 80
— 70
— 60
— 50
— 40
— 30
— 20
— 10

End 1st size
End 2nd size
End 3rd size
All sizes

ALTERNATIVE FRONT

17

NORDIC FAIR ISLE

A favourite in any yarn, this black and gold fair isle slipover has a black plain knitted back. The alternative colourways overleaf show the completely different effects that can be achieved with the same basic pattern.

■ SIZE

To fit 81[86:91]cm/32[34:36]in bust
Figures for larger sizes are given in square brackets. Where there is only one set of figures, this applies to all sizes.
See diagram for finished measurements.

■ MATERIALS

Use a fine mercerised cotton yarn.
200[225:250]g main colour A (black)
50[50:75]g 1st contrast B (sand)
50[50:75]g 2nd contrast C (beige)
50[50:75]g 3rd contrast D (grey)
One pair each of 2¾mm and 3¼mm knitting needles *or size to obtain correct tension*

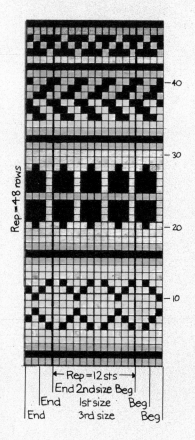

■ TENSION

32 sts and 36 rows to 10cm over fair isle patt using larger needles
31 sts and 36 rows to 10cm over st st using larger needles
Check your tension before beginning.

Note

Read chart from right to left for RS knit rows and left to right for WS purl rows. When using contrast colour, weave yarn not in use across back of work on every 2nd st.

■ FRONT

Using smaller needles and A, cast on 133[139:145] sts and work in rib as foll:
1st rib row (RS) K1, *P1, K1, rep from * to end.
2nd rib row P1, *K1, P1, rep from * to end.
Rep last 2 rows until rib measures 5cm, ending with a first row.**
Inc row P22[13:9] (M1, P44[28:21]) 2[4:6] times, M1, P23[14:10]. 136[144:152] sts.
Change to larger needles and work without shaping in fair isle patt from row 1 of chart until front measures 35[37:39]cm, ending with a WS row.

Armhole shaping

Keeping patt correct, cast off 12 sts at beg of next 2 rows. 112[120:128] sts.
Dec one st at each end of next 2 rows. 108[116:124] sts.

Neck shaping

Next row Keeping patt correct, patt 54[58:62] sts, turn and leave rem sts on a spare needle.
Dec one st at armhole edge on next and every foll alternate row *and at the same time* dec one st at neck edge on next and every foll 3rd row until

8[10:12] dec have been worked at armhole edge.
Keeping armhole edge straight cont neck shaping only until 22[24:26] sts rem.
Cont in patt without shaping until front measures 61[63:66]cm.
Cast off.
Rejoin yarn to rem 54[58:62] sts and complete to match first side, reversing shapings.

■ BACK

Using smaller needles and A, cast on 131[137:143] sts and work in rib as for front from ** to **.
Next row P, inc one st at centre of row. 132[138:144] sts.
Change to larger needles and beg with a K row, work in st st using A only until back measures same as front to armhole.

Armhole shaping

Cast off 10 sts at beg of next 2 rows. 112[118:124] sts.
Dec one st at each end of next 2 rows. 108[114:120] sts.
Dec one st at each end of next and every alternate row until 92[96:100] sts rem.
Cont without shaping until back measures 3cm less than front to shoulder, ending with a WS row.

Neck shaping

Next row (RS) K27[29:31] sts, turn and leave rem sts on a spare needle.
Dec one st at neck edge on next 5 rows. 22[24:26] sts.
Work without shaping until back measures same as front to shoulder.
Cast off.
With RS facing, rejoin yarn to rem sts, cast off centre 38 sts and work to match first side, reversing shaping.

■ NECKBAND

Join right shoulder.

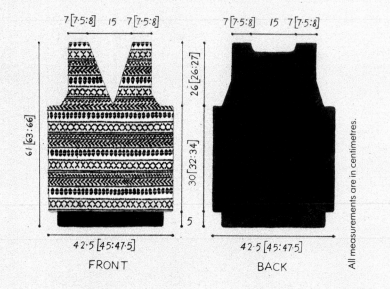

FRONT   BACK

All measurements are in centimetres.

With RS facing, using smaller needles and A, pick up and K81[84:86] sts down left front neck, one st from centre front (mark this st), 81[84:86] sts up right front neck, 6 sts down right back neck, 38 sts across back neck, 6 sts up left back neck. 213[219:223] sts.
Work in P1, K1 rib for 6 rows, dec one st at each side of centre st on every row.
Cast off evenly in rib. Join left shoulder and neckband.

■ **ARMHOLE BORDERS**
With RS facing, using smaller needles and A, pick up and K171[179:187] sts evenly around armhole.
Work in P1, K1, rib for 6 rows.
Cast off evenly in rib.

■ **MAKING UP**
Press according to instructions on yarn label.
Join side and armhole border seams.

These alternative colourways for the slipover on the preceding page all have a dominant theme of red, yet look very different, demonstrating how flexible fair isle patterns are. Choose one dominant colour or perhaps two and then select the contrasts carefully.

ZIGZAG

The special design touches – the bell frill at the neck and shoulders and the multi-coloured rib – add a touch of class to a relatively plain shape. The frill on the shoulders forms part of the sleeves, which are knitted directly onto the body of the sweater.

■ SIZE

One size to fit up to 86-97cm/34-38in bust
See diagram for finished measurements.

■ MATERIALS

Use a lightweight cotton yarn.
400g main colour A (slate)
100g contrast B (rust)
50g contrast C (pink)
50g contrast D (gold)
50g contrast E (light grey)
100g contrast F (beige)
50g contrast G (heather)
One each of 3mm and 3¾mm circular knitting needle *or size to obtain correct tension*

■ TENSION

24 sts and 30 rows to 10cm over st st using larger needle
Check your tension before beginning.

Note

Body of garment is worked in one piece to armholes.

■ WAISTBAND

Knitted as a strip in 'ridge and furrow' patt.
Using smaller needle and B, cast on 24 sts, and work in patt as foll:

1st row Using B, K.
2nd row Using B, P.
3rd row Change to A, K.
4th row Using A, K.
5th row Using A, P.
6th row Using A, K.
7th row As first row using next colour in sequence (E).
Rows 2 to 7 form patt. A is used for all 'ridges' (rows 3-6) and colours for 'furrows' are used in sequence of B,E,C,D,G,F.Cont until band measures 78cm slightly stretched, ending with a 'ridge'.
Cast off and sew up to join into a band.

■ BODY

Using larger circular needle and C, pick up and K264 sts around the less tidy edge of waistband.
Purl one round using C.
Cont without shaping, working from row 1 of body chart and using colours as indicated on colour chart, until body measures 10cm from beg of patt.

Divide for back

Next row Patt 132 sts, turn and leave rem sts on a spare needle.
Work one row.

Armhole shaping

Cast off 14 sts at beg of next 2 rows. 104 sts.
Cont in patt as set, working back and forth until armhole measures approx 30cm, ending with a 'ridge'. Leave sts on a spare needle.

■ FRONT

Rejoin yarn to rem sts and work as for back until armhole measures 23cm, ending with a WS row.

Neck shaping

Next row Patt 37 sts, turn and leave rem sts on a spare needle.
Dec one st at neck edge on every row until 27 sts rem.
Cont without shaping until front measures same as back to shoulder. Leave sts on a spare needle.
With RS facing, slip centre 30 sts onto a holder, rejoin yarn to rem sts and work to match first side, reversing shaping.

Join shoulders

Place 27 sts of front parallel with 27 sts of corresponding back shoulder with WS together and using a smaller needle and C, cast off and work picot ridge as foll:
Knit through back and front and cast

Worked in st st except for ridge rows. When working in the round, ridges are worked as K one round, P one round. When working back and forth in rows, ridges are worked as K 2 rows.

PATTERN CHART

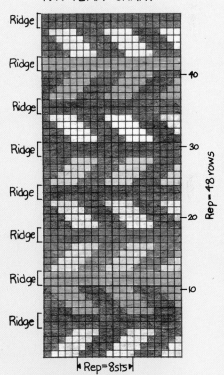

SLEEVE SHAPING

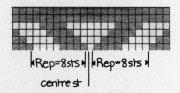

When working sleeve, slant diagonals in opposite directions on either side of centre st.
Keep patt correct on either side of centre st when decreasing.

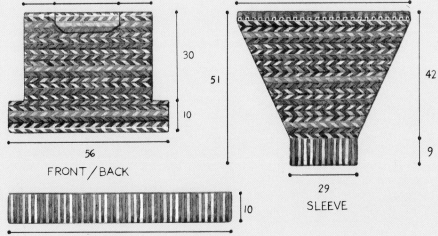

All measurements are in centimetres.

off 3 sts, *put st on RH needle back onto the front of LH needle, cast on 2 sts, K and cast off 3 sts, rep from * until all sts are cast off. Leave centre 50 sts on a holder for back neck and work other shoulder, beg at side edge.

2nd row *K5, P3, rep from * to last 6 sts, K6.
3rd row P6, *yon, K3, yrn, P5, rep from * to end.
4th row *K5, P5, rep from * to last 6 sts, K6.
5th row P6, *yon, K5, yrn, P5, rep from * to end.
6th row *K5, P7, rep from * to last 6 sts, K6.
7th row P6, *yon, K7, yrn, P5, rep from * to end.
8th row *K5, P9, rep from * to last 6 sts K6.
9th row Change to E, P6, *cast off the 8 sts of the 'bell', P5, rep from * to end. 144 sts.

10th row K, cast on one st. 145 sts. Change to larger needle and work in patt from row 1 of sleeve chart, reversing order of colours and dec either side of centre st on 3rd and every foll 4th row as foll:
3rd row Patt 70 sts, sl 1, K1, psso, K1 (centre st), K2tog, patt rem 70 sts.
7th row Patt 69 sts, sl 1, K1, psso, K1 (centre st), K2tog, patt rem 69 sts.
Cont dec as set until sleeve measures approx 42cm from 'ridge' in colour C at beg, ending with a complete patt.
Next row Using C, K, dec evenly to 56 sts. Cast off in C.

■ SLEEVES (Make 2)
With RS facing and using larger needle and C, pick up and K144 sts evenly around armhole.
Knit one row.
Change to smaller needle and A, knit one row.
Next row *K5, P1, rep from * to end.
Work bell frill as foll:
1st row (RS) P6, *yon, K1, yrn, P5, rep from * to end.

■ CUFFS (Make 2)
With RS facing and using smaller needle and B, cast on 20 sts and work as for waistband until 15 ridges are completed.
Cast off on 4th row of 15th ridge.

■ NECKBAND
With RS facing and using smaller circular needle and E, K50 sts from back neck, pick up and K17 sts down left side of neck, K30 sts from front neck and pick up and K17 sts up right side of neck. 114 sts.
Make frill as foll:
1st round P3, *cast on 8 by twisting yarn onto RH needle with left thumb, P6, rep from * to last 3 sts, cast on 8, P3.
2nd round Change to A, P3, *K8, P6, rep from * to last 11 sts, K8, P3.
3rd round As 2nd round.
4th round P3, *sl 1, K1, psso, K4, K2tog, P6, rep from * to last 11 sts, sl 1, K1, psso, K4, K2tog, P3.
5th round P3, *K6, P6, rep from * to last 9 sts, K6, P3.
6th round P3, *sl 1, K1, psso, K2, K2tog, P6, rep from * to last 9 sts, sl 1, K1, psso, K2, K2tog, P3.
7th round P3, *K4, P6, rep from * to last 7 sts, K4, P3.
8th round P3, *sl 1, K1, psso, K2tog, P6, rep from * to last 7 sts, sl 1, K1, psso, K2tog, P3.
9th round P3, *K2, P6, rep from * to last 5 sts, K2, P3.
10th round P3, *K2tog, P6, rep from * to last 5 sts, K2tog, P3.
11th round P3, *K1, P6, rep from * to last 4 sts, K1, P3.
12th round P3, *K2tog, P5, rep from * to last 4 sts, K2tog, P2. 114 sts.
13th round Using C, K. Cast off.

■ MAKING UP
Sew cuffs to lower edge of sleeve, stretching to fit.
Sew sleeve to cast off sts at underarm and join sleeve seam.
Press according to instructions on yarn label.

ICE COOL

Fine lightweight cotton and a flattering cut away shoulder line make this a perfect summer top. A variation of the same cable pattern can be adapted to a boat neck top in a fancy cotton and silk yarn.

■ SIZE
One size to fit up to 97cm/38in bust
See diagram for finished measurements.

■ MATERIALS
250g fine cotton yarn for vest version
400g fine cotton fancy yarn for boat neck version
One pair each of 2¾mm and 3mm knitting needles *or size to obtain correct tension*
One cable needle

■ TENSION
16 sts and 16 rows to 10cm over st st using larger needles
Check your tension before beginning.

■ BACK
**Using smaller needles, cast on 119 sts and work in rib as foll:
1st rib row (RS) K1, *P1, K1, rep from * to end.
2nd rib row P1, *K1, P1, rep from * to end.
Rep last 2 rows until rib measures 5cm, ending with a 2nd rib row and inc one st in last row. 120 sts.
Change to larger needles and work in patt as foll:
1st row K1, slip first st onto cable needle and leave at front of work, K1, then K1 from cable needle, – called T2 –, (K winding yarn around needle twice – called KW) 24 times, (K6, KW24) 3 times, T2, K1.
2nd and every alternate row P3, K24, (P6, K24) 3 times, P3.

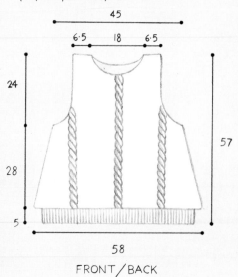

FRONT / BACK

All measurements are in centimetres.

24

3rd row As first row.
5th row K1, T2, KW24, slip next 3 sts onto cable needle and leave at front of work, K3, then K3 from cable needle – called C6 –, (KW24, C6) twice, KW24, T2, K1.
7th row As first row.
8th row As 2nd row.
**Cont in patt as set *and at the same time* keeping 3 edge sts correct, dec one st at each end of next and every foll 7th row (3 sts in) until 92 sts rem (keeping cable panels correct).
Cont without shaping until back measures 33cm, ending with a WS row.

Armhole shaping
Cast off 5 sts at beg of next 2 rows.
Keeping 3 edge sts correct, dec one st (3 sts in) at each end of next and every foll 3rd row until 60 sts rem.
Cont without shaping until back measures 52cm.

Back neck shaping
Patt 19 sts, turn and leave rem sts on a spare needle.
Next row P3, K to last 3 sts, P3.
Keeping 3 edge sts correct, dec one st at neck edge (3 sts in) on next and 5 foll alternate rows.
Work one row.
Cast off rem 13 sts.
With RS facing, rejoin yarn to rem sts, cast off centre 22 sts and work to match first side, reversing all shaping.

■ **FRONT**
Work as for back until front measures 48cm.

Front neck shaping
Next row Patt 21 sts, turn and leave rem sts on a spare needle.
Next row P3, K to last 3 sts, P3.
Keeping 3 edge sts correct dec one st at neck edge (3 sts in) on next and 7 foll alternate rows. 13 sts.
Work a few rows without shaping until front measures same as back to shoulder.
Cast off.
With RS facing, rejoin yarn to rem sts, cast off centre 18 sts and work to match first side, reversing all shaping.

■ **NECKBAND**
Join right shoulder seam.
With RS facing and using smaller needles, pick up and K25 sts down left front, K18 sts across centre front, K25 sts up right front, K16 sts down right back neck, K22 across centre back and K15 sts up left back neck. 121 sts.
Work in rib as for back for 5 rows.
Cast off loosely in rib.

■ **ARMHOLE BANDS** (Make 2)
Join left shoulder and neckband seam.
With RS facing and using smaller needles, pick up and K111 sts evenly around armhole.
Work in rib as for back for 5 rows.
Cast off loosely in rib.

■ **MAKING UP**
Join side and armband seams.

BOAT NECK SHIRT

■ **BACK AND FRONT** (Both alike)
Work as for back of vest from ** to **.
Keeping the 3 edge sts correct, cont in patt as set until work measures 33cm, ending with a WS row.

Armhole shaping
Cast off 5 sts at beg of next 2 rows. 110 sts.
Keeping 3 edge sts correct, cont

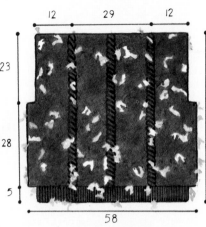

without shaping until work measures 56cm.
Cast off.

■ **MAKING UP**
Join shoulders for 12cm.
Join side seams.

All measurements are in centimetres.

FRONT / BACK

JANICE WILKINS

MONDRIAN SQUARES

A simple shape provides the canvas for these Mondrian-style blocks of colour. The neat shirt collar and classic shape would suit any member of the family. Try alternative colourways to suit different personalities.

■ SIZE
To fit 81-86[91-97]cm/32-34 [36-38]in bust
Figures for larger sizes are given in square brackets. Where there is only one set of figures, this applies to all sizes.
See diagram for finished measurements.

■ MATERIALS
Use a mediumweight cotton yarn.
620[650]g main colour A (white)
30[40]g 1st contrast B (black)
100[120]g 2nd contrast C (yellow)
One pair each of 3¾mm and 4½mm knitting needles *or size to obtain correct tension*

■ TENSION
17 sts and 25 rows to 10cm over moss st using larger needles
Check your tension before beginning.

Note
Read chart from right to left for RS odd numbered rows and left to right for even numbered rows.
Use separate balls of yarn for each area. Do not carry yarn not in use across back of work (see page 114).

■ STITCHES
Moss st (Main colour A only)
Worked over even number of sts.
1st row *K1, P1, rep from * to end.
2nd row *P1, K1, rep from * to end.
These 2 rows form patt.
Worked over odd number of sts.
1st row K1, *P1, K1, rep from * to end.
This row forms patt.

Stocking st (B and C only)
1st row (RS) K.
2nd row P.
These 2 rows form patt.

■ BACK
Using smaller needles, cast on 81[93] sts as foll:
20[26]A, 1B, 19A, 1B, 19A, 1B, 20[26]A.
Keeping to colours as set, work in rib as foll:
1st rib row K1, *P1, K1, rep from * to end.
2nd rib row P1, *K1, P1, rep from * to end.
Rep last 2 rows until rib measures 8cm, ending with a first row.

First size only:
Inc row Rib 5, (M1 , rib 5) 3 times, [rib 4, (M1, rib 4) 4 times] twice, rib 6 (M1, rib 5) 3 times. 95 sts.
2nd size only:
Inc row (Rib 5, M1) 5 times, rib 5, (M1, rib 4) 4 times, (rib 4, M1) 4 times, (rib 6, M1) 4 times, rib 7. 110 sts.
Both sizes:
Change to larger needles and work without shaping in patts from chart, ensuring colour B continues in correct position.
Place marker at each end of row 65[79] for armholes.
When chart is complete cast off.

■ FRONT
Work as for back to end of row 120[134].

Neck shaping
Next row Patt 42[49] sts, turn and leave rem sts on a spare needle. Cast off 2 sts at neck edge on next 5 rows. 32[39] sts.
Cont without shaping until front matches back to shoulder.
Cast off.
Rejoin yarn to rem sts, cast off centre 11[12] sts and work to match first side, reversing shaping.

■ SLEEVES (Make 2)
Using larger needles, cast on 38 sts as foll:
19A, 1B, 18A.
Work in patt of A in moss st and B in st st without shaping for 36 rows.
Now work from chart, shaping sides by inc one st at each end of 4th and every foll 3rd row until there are 96 sts.
Cont without shaping for 12 rows to end of sleeve chart.
Cast off.

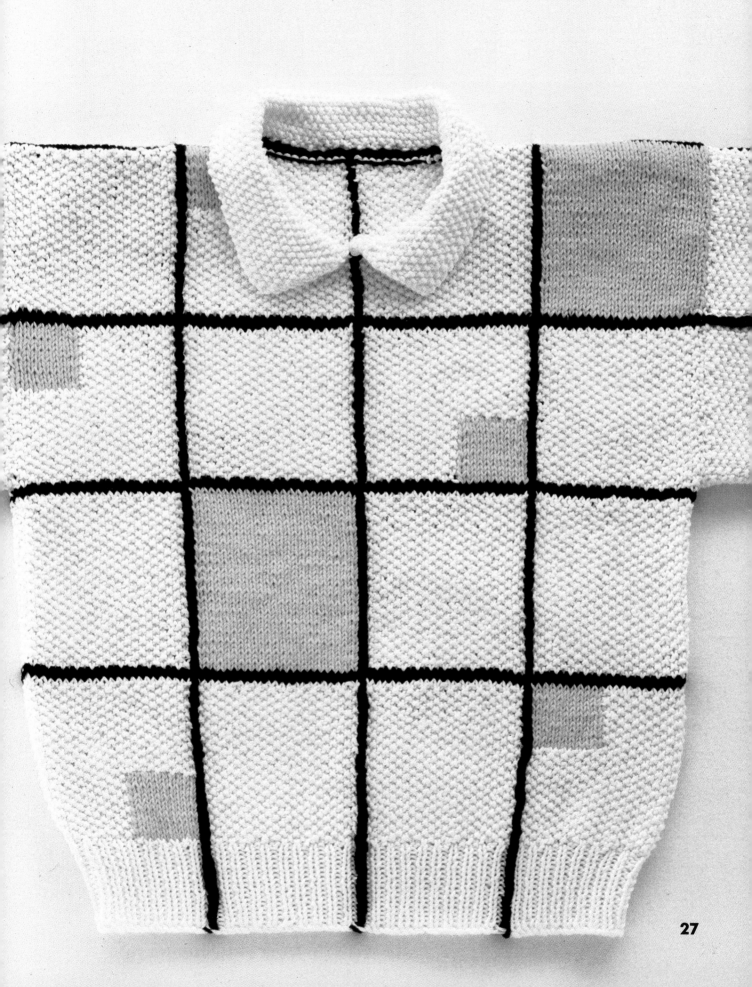

■ COLLAR

Using larger needles and A, cast on 14 sts and work in moss st for 128 rows. Cast off.

■ MAKING UP

Press according to instructions on yarn label.
Join shoulder seams.
Sew cast off edge of sleeves to back and front between markers.
Join side and sleeve seams.
Sew row ends of collar to neck edge.

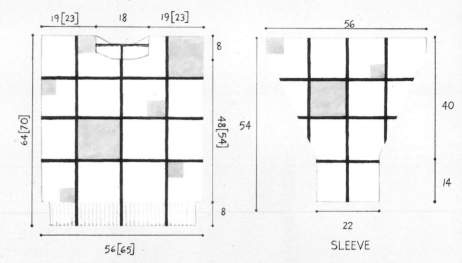

19 [23]   18   19 [23]
8
64 [70]   48 [54]   54
8
56 [65]

FRONT / BACK

56
40
14
22
SLEEVE

All measurements are in centimetres.

This shape and design can easily be altered to change its appeal and personality. It works well no matter which way you use the colours: it is equally effective if you reverse the black, neutral and brown or use three strong colours together, such as purple, black and pink.

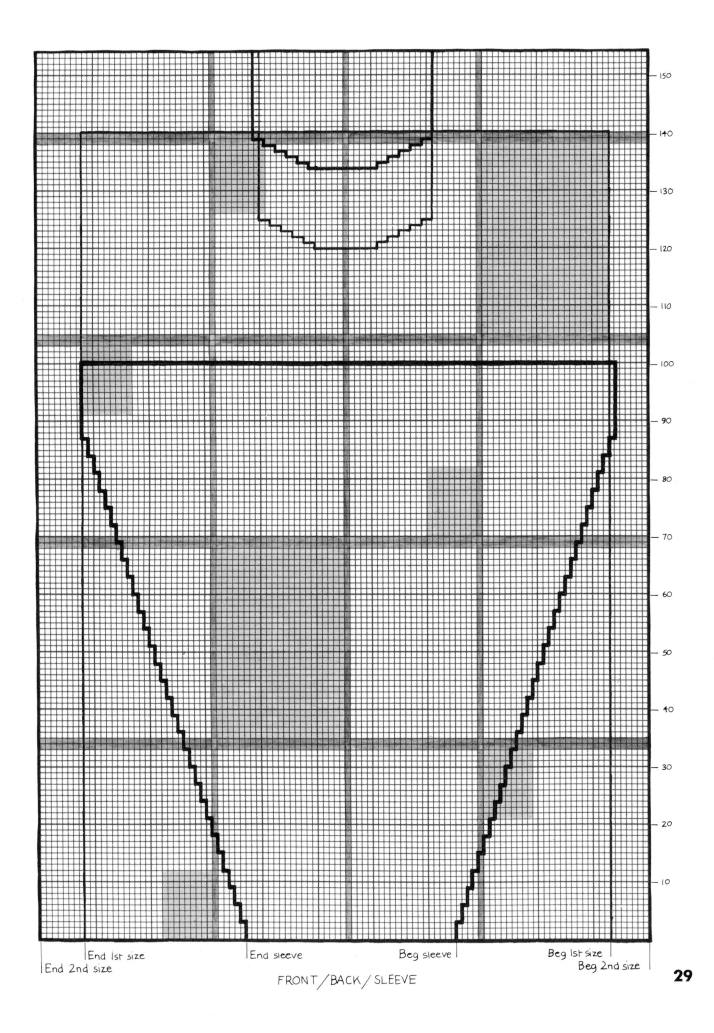

End 2nd size

End 1st size

End sleeve

Beg sleeve

Beg 1st size

Beg 2nd size

FRONT / BACK / SLEEVE

150

140

130

120

110

100

90

80

70

60

50

40

30

20

10

FINESSE

This beautifully crafted long-line classic has a lace pattern knitted within a twisted stitch panel on the body and the sleeves. A smaller lace pattern is provided on page 32.

■ SIZE

To fit 81-86[91:102]cm/32-34[36:38-40]in bust
Figures for larger sizes are given in square brackets. Where there is only one set of figures, this applies to all sizes.
See diagram for finished measurements.

■ MATERIALS

550[600:650]g fine mercerised cotton yarn
One pair each of 2¾mm and 3¼mm knitting needles *or size to obtain correct tension*
One cable needle

■ TENSION

28 sts and 40 rows to 10cm over st st using larger needles
Check your tension before beginning.

■ BACK

Using smaller needles, cast on 110[114:118] sts and work in rib as foll:
1st rib row (RS) K2, *P2, K2, rep from * to end.
2nd rib row P2, *K2, P2, rep from * to end.
Rep last 2 rows until rib measures 15cm, ending with a WS row.
Inc row Rib 3, (M1, rib 4) 10[6:2] times, (M1, rib 3) 9[21:33] times, (M1, rib 4) 10[6:2] times. 139[147:155] sts.
Change to larger needles and work in patt as foll:
1st row K13[17:21], (P1, K11) 3 times, P1, K1 tbl, P1, slip next 3 sts onto cable needle, turn cable needle and knit 3rd, 2nd and first st – called T3 –, P1, K1 tbl, P1, †K11, yfwd, K2tog, K10, †P1, K1 tbl, P1, T3, P1, K1 tbl, P1, (K11, P1) 3 times, K13[17:21].
2nd row and every alternate row P.
3rd row K13[17:21], (P1, K11) 3 times, P1, K1 tbl, P1, K3, P1, K1 tbl, P1, †K9, K2tog, yfwd, K1, yfwd, sl 1, K1, psso, K9, †P1, K1 tbl, P1, K3, P1, K1 tbl, P1, (K11, P1) 3 times, K13[17:21].
5th row K13[17:21], (P1, K11) 3 times, P1, K1 tbl, P1, T3, P1, K1 tbl, P1, †K8, K2tog, yfwd, K3, yfwd, sl 1, K1, psso, K8, †P1, K1 tbl, P1, T3, P1, K1 tbl, P1, (K11, P1) 3 times, K13[17:21].
7th row K13[17:21], (P1, K11) 3 times, P1, K1 tbl, P1, K3, P1, K1 tbl, P1, †K7, K2tog, yfwd, K5, yfwd, sl 1, K1, psso, K7, †P1, K1 tbl, P1, K3, P1, K1 tbl, P1,

(K11, P1) 3 times, K13[17:21].
9th row K13[17:21], (P1, K11) 3 times, P1, K1 tbl, P1, T3, P1, K1 tbl, P1, †K6 K2tog, yfwd, K7, yfwd, sl 1, K1, psso K6, †P1, K1 tbl, P1, T3, P1, K1 tbl, P1, (K11, P1) 3 times, K13[17:21].
11th row K13[17:21], (P1, K11) 3 times, P1, K1 tbl, P1, K3, P1, K1 tbl, P1, K5, K2tog, yfwd, K9, yfwd, sl 1, K1, psso, K5, †P1, K1 tbl, P1, K3, P1, K1 tbl, P1, (K11, P1) 3 times, K13[17:21].
13th row K13[17:21], (P1, K11) 3 times, P1, K1 tbl, P1, T3, P1, K1 tbl, P1, †K4, K2tog, yfwd, K11, yfwd, sl 1, K1, psso, K4, †P1, K1 tbl, P1, T3, P1, K1 tbl, P1, (K11, P1) 3 times, K13[17:21].
15th row K13[17:21], (P1, K11) 3 times, P1, K1 tbl, P1, K3, P1, K1 tbl, P1, †K3, K2tog, yfwd, K13, yfwd, sl 1, K1, psso, K3, †P1, K1 tbl, P1, K3, P1, K1 tbl, P1, (K11, P1) 3 times, K13[17:21].
17th row K13[17:21], (P1, K11) 3 times, P1, K1 tbl, P1, T3, P1, K1 tbl, P1, †K2, K2tog, yfwd, K15, yfwd, sl 1, K1, psso, K2, †P1, K1 tbl, P1, T3, P1, K1 tbl, P1, (K11, P1) 3 times, K13[17:21].
19th row K13[17:21], (P1, K11) 3 times, P1, K1 tbl, P1, K3, P1, K1 tbl, P1, †K1, K2tog, yfwd, K17, yfwd, sl 1, K1, psso, K1, †P1, K1 tbl, P1, K3, P1, K1 tbl, P1, (K11, P1) 3 times, K13[17:21].
21st row K13[17:21], (P1, K11) 3 times, P1, K1 tbl, P1, T3, P1, K1 tbl, P1, †K23, †P1, K1 tbl, P1, T3, P1, K1 tbl, P1, (K11, P1) 3 times, K13[17:21].
23rd row K13[17:21], (P1, K11) 3 times, P1, K1 tbl, P1, K3, P1, K1 tbl, P1, †K23, †P1, K1 tbl, P1, K3, P1, K1 tbl, P1, (K11, P1) 3 times, K13[17:21].
24th row As 2nd row.
These 24 rows form patt.
Cont without shaping in patt until back measures 56[61:66]cm, ending with a WS row.

Divide for back opening

Next row Patt 69[73:77] sts, turn and leave rem sts on a spare needle.
Cont without shaping until back measures 66[71:76]cm, ending with a RS row.

Neck shaping

Next row Cast off 15[16:17] sts, patt to end.
Dec one st at neck edge on every foll row until 46[49:52] sts rem.
Cont without shaping until back measures 71[76:81]cm, ending with a WS row.
Cast off.
With RS facing rejoin yarn to rem sts, K2 tog, patt to end.
Work to match first side, reversing shaping.

■ FRONT

Work as for back until front measures 61[66:71]cm *without* dividing sts for back opening, ending with a WS row.

Neck shaping

Next row Patt 56[59:62] sts, turn and leave rem sts on a spare needle.
Dec one st at neck edge on every foll row until 46[49:52] sts rem.
Cont without shaping until front measures 71[76:81]cm.
Cast off.
With RS facing, rejoin yarn to rem sts and cast off centre 27[29:31] sts, patt to end.
Work to match first side, reversing shaping.

■ SLEEVES (Make 2)

Using smaller needles, cast on 58 sts and work in rib as for back until sleeve measures 5cm, ending with a RS row.
Inc row Rib 3, (M1, rib 4) 5 times, (M1, rib 3) 5 times, (m1, rib 4) 5 times. 73 sts.
Change to larger needles and patt, placing first row as foll:
1st row K4, P1, K11, P1, K1 tbl, P1, T3, P1, K1 tbl, P1, †K11, yfwd, K2tog, K10, †P1, K1 tbl, P1, T3, P1, K1 tbl, P1, K11, P1, K4.
Cont in patt as set working lace panel in centre of sleeve and one rib only at each side *and at the same time* shape sides by inc one st at each end of 3rd and every 4th row until there are 153 sts, working all inc sts in st st.

Cont without shaping until sleeve measures 48cm, ending with a WS row.
Next row (RS) P.
Cast off.

■ BACK BUTTONHOLE BAND
With RS facing and using smaller needles, pick up and K32 sts up left edge of back opening.
Next row *K10, yrn, K2tog, rep from * once, K to end.
Next row K.
Cast off.

■ BACK BUTTONBAND
Work as for buttonhole band omitting buttonholes.

■ NECKBAND
Join shoulder seams.
With RS facing and using smaller needles, pick up and K35 sts up left back neck, 34 sts down left front neck, 26[28:30] sts across front, 34 sts up right front neck, 35 sts down right back neck. 164[166:168] sts.
Next row K to last 4 sts, K2tog, yrn, K2.
Next row K.
Cast off.

■ MAKING UP
Fold cast off edge of sleeves in half and place this point to shoulder seam.
Sew edge of sleeves to front and back.
Ensure that purl row on sleeves is showing on right side of work.
Join side and sleeve seams.
Sew on buttons.
Press according to instructions on yarn label.

The samples show the small lace V pattern in grey and the original pattern in salmon pink.

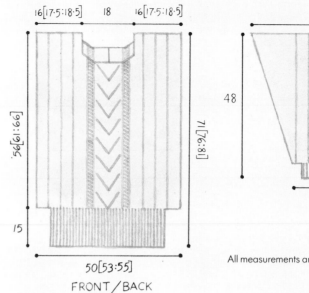

FRONT/BACK

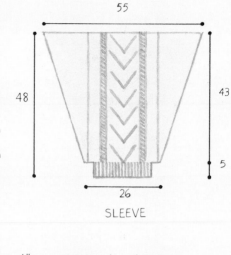

SLEEVE

All measurements are in centimetres.

LACE PANEL VARIATION

This classic sweater can be given a different look by knitting a smaller version of the lace stitch. All you need to do is replace the stitches between † and † in the main pattern with the following pattern.

■ SMALL LACE V
1st row K11, yfwd, K2tog, K10.
2nd row and every alternate row P.
3rd row K9, K2tog, yfwd, K1, yfwd, sl 1, K1, psso, K9.

5th row K8, K2tog, yfwd, K3, yfwd, sl 1, K1, psso, K8.
7th row K7, K2tog, yfwd, K5, yfwd, sl 1, K1, psso, K7.
9th, 11th, 13th, 15th rows K.
These 16 rows form patt.

BALLOONS

The pastel colours within the balloon shapes on this long sweater are knitted in five tones so that balloons seem to rise against the natural background. Reducing the length and leaving off the rib converts the design into a T-shirt.

SIZE

One size to fit up to 91cm/36in bust
See diagram for finished measurements.

MATERIALS

Use a lightweight cotton yarn double throughout and light and medium weight yarns for contrast.
600g main colour A (300g white, 300g cream – natural)

250g 1st contrast B (100g dark, 50g medium, 50g light & 50g pale orange)
350g 2nd contrast C (150g dark, 100g medium, 50g light & 50g pale pink)
350g 3rd contrast D (100g dark, 100g medium, 100g light & 50g pale green)
200g 4th contrast E (50g dark, 50g medium, 50g light & 50g pale turquoise)
350g 5th contrast F (50g dark, 100g medium, 100g light & 100g pale blue)
One pair each of 4½mm and 6mm knitting needles (or circular knitting needle if preferred) *or size to obtain correct tension*
One 2.50mm crochet hook

TENSION

15 sts and 19 rows to 10cm over st st using larger needles
Check your tension before beginning.

Note

Use separate balls of yarn for each area, do not carry yarn across back of work. Take care to twist yarns at the back when changing colours to avoid holes forming(see page 114).
Read chart from right to left for RS knit rows and left to right for WS purl rows. Unless stated st st is used throughout. This garment is worked in one piece. The colours of each balloon are indicated on the layout of the dress. The yarns are then used either double or two mixed to achieve the 4 tones for each motif.
The background yarn is used either double or mixed so as to give as much variation in colour and texture as possible.

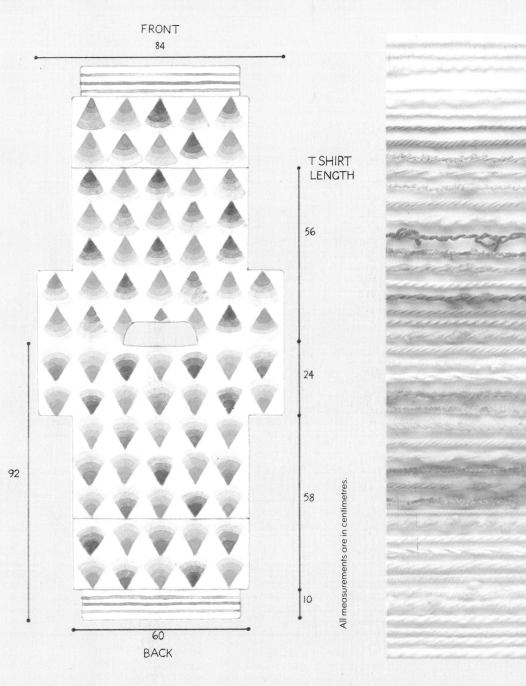

FRONT

84

T SHIRT LENGTH

56

24

58

10

92

60

BACK

All measurements are in centimetres.

■ BODY

Back

Using smaller needles and natural, cast on 77 sts and work in rib as foll:
1st rib row (RS) K1, *P1, K1, rep from * to end.
2nd rib row P1, *K1, P1, rep from * to end.
Rep last 2 rows for 27 rows, working next 3 rows in natural, 3 rows in med blue, 5 rows natural, 3 rows med pink, 5 rows natural, 3 rows med green and 5 rows natural, ending with a first row.
Inc row Using natural, rib 6 (M1, rib 6) 3 times, (M1, rib 5) 7 times, (M1, rib 6) 3 times. 90 sts.
Change to larger needles and work without shaping from chart, rep rows 1 to 44 until the end of row 106.

Sleeve shaping

Cast on 18 sts at beg of next 2 rows. 126 sts.
Cont without shaping until end of row 154.

Back neck shaping

Next row Patt 51 sts, turn and leave rem sts on a spare needle.
Next row Cast off 7 sts, patt to end. 44 sts. (This row forms top of shoulder.)

Work 4 rows without shaping, working down graph from row 24 (so that the balloons are reversed).

Front neck shaping

**Inc one st at neck edge on next row.
Cast on 2 sts at beg of next row.
Work one row.
Cast on 3 sts at beg of next row.
Work one row.
Cast on 5 sts at beg of next row.**
Work one row. 55 sts.
Rejoin yarn to rem sts, cast off centre 24 sts and patt to end.
Work one row. Cast off 7 sts at beg of next row, patt to end. 44 sts. Work 4 rows without shaping. Rep from ** to ** as first side, ending with a K row.
Next row P to end, turn and cast on 16 sts, turn and P sts from spare needle. 126 sts.
Cont without shaping until 50 rows have been worked from top of shoulder.

Sleeve shaping

Cast off 18 sts at beg of next 2 rows. 90 sts.
Cont without shaping until front matches back, ending with row 24 of patt.

Next row (K2tog, P1, [K1, P1] twice) 12 times, K2tog, (P1, K1) twice. 77 sts.
Work rib in stripes as for back.
Cast off loosely in rib.

■ SLEEVE EDGES

With RS facing and using smaller needles and natural, pick up and K91 sts evenly along edge of sleeve.
Knit one row.
Work 8 rows in st st, beg with a K row.
Cast off loosely.

■ NECK EDGING

Using 2.50mm crochet hook and natural yarn singly, work one row of double crochet evenly around neck edge.

■ MAKING UP

Press lightly on WS, avoiding ribs.
Join side and sleeve seams.
Catch down sleeve edges onto WS to hem sleeve.

T-SHIRT VERSION

■ BODY

Work as for dress version, omitting rib rows from ** to ** and omitting first 2 rows of balloons.

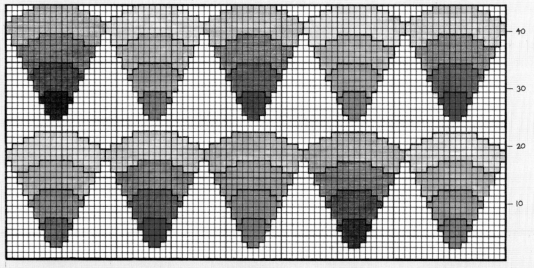

PATTERN CHART

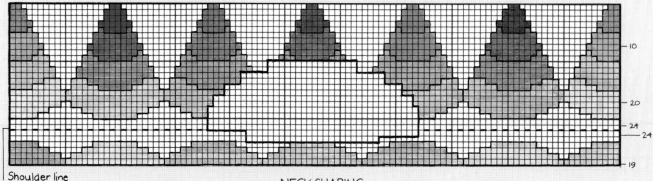

Shoulder line

NECK SHAPING

SPORTING STRIPES

Clear blue and white stripes give a sporty feeling to this loose shirt-style sweater. You could adapt it by knitting in wider stripes, using more colour combinations or knitting the rib, band and collar in a single colour.

■ SIZE
One size to fit up to 97cm/38in bust
See diagram for finished measurements.

■ MATERIALS
Use a lightweight cotton slub yarn.
400g colour A (blue)
400g colour B (white)
One pair each of 2¾mm and 3mm knitting needles *or size to obtain correct tension*
Three 15mm buttons

■ TENSION
32 sts and 32 rows to 10cm over patt using larger needles
Check your tension before beginning.

■ BACK
Using smaller needles and B, cast on 168 sts and work in rib as foll:
1st rib row *K3A, P3B, rep from * to end.
2nd rib row *K3B, P3A, rep from * to end.
Rep last 2 rows 3 times.
Change to larger needles and work in patt as foll:
1st row *K3B, K3A, rep from * to end.
2nd row P1B, *P3A, P3B, rep from * to last 5 sts, P3A, P2B.
3rd row K1B, *K3A, K3B, rep from * to last 5 sts, K3A, K2B.
4th row *P3B, P3A, rep from * to end.
5th row K2A, *K3B, K3A, rep from * to last 4 sts, K3B, K1A,
6th row P2A, *P3B, P3A, rep from * to last 4 sts, P3B, P1A.
These 6 rows form patt.
Cont in patt without shaping until back measures 43cm, ending with a WS row.

Armhole shaping
Cast off 8 sts at beg of next 2 rows. 152 sts.
Cont without shaping until back measures 62cm, ending with a WS row.

Neck shaping
Next row Patt 56 sts, turn and leave rem sts on a spare needle.
Dec one st at neck edge on next and 3 foll alternate rows. 52 sts.
Cast off using A.
With RS facing, rejoin yarn to rem sts, cast off centre 40 sts, patt to end.
Work to match first side, reversing shaping.

■ FRONT
Work as for back until front measures 37.5cm, ending with a WS row.

Front opening
Next row Patt 80 sts, pick up 8 sts for buttonband by picking up loop of previous row at back of next 8 sts, turn and leave rem sts on a spare needle. 88 sts.
Working these 8 sts in K1A, P1B rib and rem sts in patt, cont without shaping until front matches back to armhole, ending with a WS row.

Armhole shaping
Cast off 8 sts at beg of next row. 80 sts.
Cont without shaping in patts as set until front measures 36 rows less than back, ending with a RS row.

Neck shaping
Cast off 16 sts at beg of next row. 64 sts.
Dec one st at neck edge of next and 5 foll alternate rows. 58 sts.
Work 3 rows.
Dec one st at neck edge of next and 5 foll 4th rows. 52 sts.
Cast off using A.
Mark positions for 3 buttons on buttonband.
Rejoin yarn to rem 88 sts and work to match first side, reversing shapings and working 3 buttonholes opposite button positions as foll:
1st buttonhole row Rib 3, cast off 2 sts, rib to end.
2nd buttonhole row Rib, casting on 2 sts over those cast off on previous row.

■ SLEEVES (Make 2)
Using smaller needles and B, cast on 66 sts and work in rib as for back for 6cm, inc one st in last row. 67 sts.
Change to larger needles and cont in patt as set, shaping sides by inc one st at each end of every 3rd row until there are 155 sts and sleeve measures approx 48cm.

Top shaping
Dec one st at each end of next and 3 foll alternate rows. 147 sts.
Cast off using A.

■ COLLAR
Join shoulder seams.
With RS facing and A, pick up and K41 sts up right front neck, 61 sts around back neck and 41 sts down left front neck omitting tops of bands. 143 sts.
Work in K1A, P1B rib as for buttonband for 7cm.
Cast off loosely in rib using A.

◾ POCKET

Using larger needles and B, cast on 40 sts and work 13cm in diagonal stripe patt.
Change to smaller needles and work in K1A, P1B rib for 2cm.
Cast off loosely in rib using A.

◾ MAKING UP

Press according to instructions on yarn label.
Place centre of cast off edge of sleeve to shoulder seam and join to back and front.
Join side and sleeve seams.
Sew on pocket in desired position.
Sew on buttons.

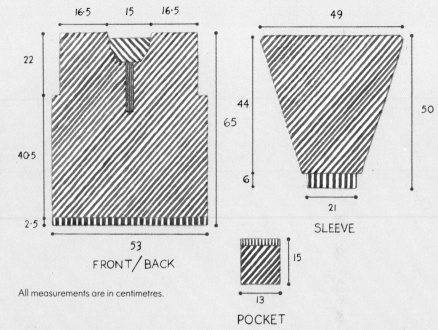

FRONT/BACK

SLEEVE

POCKET

All measurements are in centimetres.

STRIPE VARIATION

You could make the stripe wider by knitting six stitches in each diagonal stripe instead of three. If so, the first row of the back will then be worked as *K6B, K6A, rep from * to end. Or you can change the colourway by using more than two colours: here the master pattern has been knitted up in grey, yellow and white. By using three colours, with the yarn woven in at the back of the work, a tighter, thicker fabric is created and consequently a warmer one.

CABLE CLASSIC

An elegant classic shape with a cable, this cardigan is a timeless design that would suit almost anybody.

■ SIZE

To fit 81-86[91-97:102-107]cm/32-34[36-38:40-42]in bust
Figures for larger sizes are given in square brackets. Where there is only one set of figures, this applies to all sizes.
See diagram for finished measurements.

■ MATERIALS

500[550:600]g fine mercerised cotton yarn
One pair each of 2¾mm and 3¼mm knitting needles *or size to obtain correct tension*
Four 15mm buttons
One cable needle

■ TENSION

28 sts and 38 rows to 10cm over st st using larger needles
Check your tension before beginning.

Note

Slip first stitch and knit last stitch on every row to ensure a firm edge.

■ BACK

Using smaller needles, cast on 121[127:133] sts.
1st rib row (RS) K to end, working into back of every st.
2nd rib row P1, *K1, P1, rep from * to end.
3rd rib row K1, P1, K1, rep from * to end.
Rep last 2 rows until rib measures 10cm, ending with a 3rd row.**
Inc row P4, (M1, P4) 4[6:8] times, (M1, P5) 17[15:13] times, (M1, P4) 4[6:8] times.146[154:162] sts.
Change to larger needles and work in patt as foll:
1st row (RS) K13[17:21], *P3, K9, P3*, K90, rep from * to * once, K13[17:21].
2nd row and every alternate row P13[17:21], *K1, P1, K1, P9, K1, P1, K1*, P90, rep from * to * once, P13[17:21].
3rd row K13[17:21], *P3, slip 3 sts onto cable needle and hold at front of work, K3, then K3 from cable needle — called CF6 –, K3, P3*, K90, rep from * to * once, K13[17:21].
5th row As first row.
7th row K13[17:21], *P3, K3, slip 3 sts onto cable needle and hold at back of work, K3, then K3 from cable needle –

An alternative pastel colourway (in the same mercerised cotton) to the pale green used in the main pattern overleaf.

called CB6 –, P3*, K90, rep from * to * once, K13[17:21].
8th row As 2nd row.
These 8 rows form patt.
Cont in patt without shaping until back measures 60[65:70]cm, ending with a RS row.
Cast off.

■ RIGHT FRONT

Using smaller needles, cast on 49[51:53] sts and work as for back from ** to **.
Inc row P3, (M1, P4) 5[3:1] times, (M1, P3) 2[8:14] times, (M1, P4) 5[3:1] times. 61[65:69] sts.
Change to larger needles and work in patt as foll:
1st row K33, P3, K9, P3, K13[17:21].

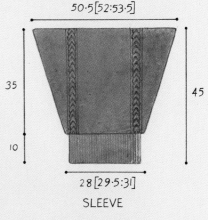

50·5[52:53·5]

35

45

10

28[29·5:31]

SLEEVE

All measurements are in centimetres.

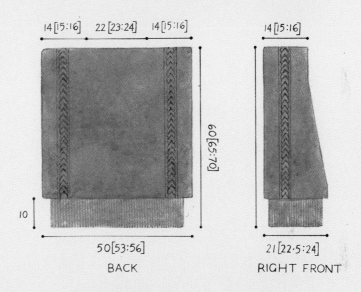

14[15:16]   22[23:24]   14[15:16]

60[65:70]

10

50[53:56]

BACK

14[15:16]

21[22·5:24]

RIGHT FRONT

39

2nd and every alternate row
P13[17:21], K1, P1, K1, P9, K1, P1, K1, P33.
3rd row K33, P3, C6F, K3, P3, K13[17:21].
5th row As first row.
7th row K33, P3, K3, C6B, P3, K13[17:21].
8th row As 2nd row.
These 8 rows form patt.
Cont in patt without shaping until front measures 13cm, ending with a RS row.

Front shaping
Dec one st at beg of next and every foll 8th row until 43[45:47] sts rem.
Cont without shaping until front measures 60[65:70]cm.
Cast off.

■ LEFT FRONT
Work as for right front, reversing shaping and placing first row of patt as foll:
1st row K13[17:21], P3, K9, P3, K33.

■ SLEEVES (Make 2)
Using smaller needles, cast on 59 sts and work as back from ** to **.
Inc row P3, (M1, P1) 0[3:7] times, (M1, P2) 26[24:20] times, (M1, P1) 0[3:7] times, P4[2:2]. 85[89:93] sts.
Change to larger needles and work in patt as for back, placing first row as foll:
1st row K3, *P3, K9, P3*, K49[53:57], rep from * to * once, K3.
Cont in patt, shaping sides by inc one st at each end of 3rd and every foll 4th

row until there are 147[151:155] sts, working extra sts in st st.
Work without shaping until sleeve measures 45cm, ending with a WS row.
Next row (RS) P.
Cast off.

■ FRONT BANDS AND COLLAR
Using smaller needles, cast on 39 sts.
1st row (RS) K to end, working into back of every st.
2nd row K2, *P1, K1, rep from * to last st, K1.
3rd row K1, *P1, K1, rep from * to end.
Rep last 2 rows twice.
1st buttonhole row Rib 8, cast off 2 sts, rib 19, cast off 2 sts, rib 8.
2nd buttonhole row Rib, casting on 2 sts over those cast off on previous row.
Cont in rib until band measures 13cm.
Work the 2 buttonhole rows once more.
Cont in rib until band when slightly stretched fits up right front, across back neck and down left front.
Cast off.

■ MAKING UP
Join shoulder seams.
Mark central point of back neck and ribbed collar.
Place collar at centre of back neck and sew evenly to right and left fronts with buttonholes at bottom of right front.
Place centre of cast off edge of sleeves to shoulder seams and join sleeves to back and front evenly.
Join side and sleeve seams.
Sew on buttons.
Press according to instructions on yarn label.

41

CABBAGE ROSE

The simple scattered motif of a cabbage rose on a classic raglan sweater offers possibilities for completely different effects, depending on the yarns chosen. The fleck yarn has an earthy appeal, while a white yarn creates a more sophisticated look (see page 46).

■ SIZE
To fit 86[91:97-102]cm/34[36:38-40]in bust
Figures for larger sizes are given in square brackets. Where there is only one set of figures, this applies to all sizes.
See diagram for finished measurements.

■ MATERIALS
Use a fine cotton yarn knitted double for the main colour and a medium weight cotton yarn for contrast.
700[750:800]g main colour A (brown fleck)
70g contrast B (green)
25g each C, D, E and F (blue, yellow, pink, beige)
One pair each of 3¼mm and 4½mm knitting needles *or size to obtain correct tension*

■ TENSION
18 sts and 26 rows to 10cm over st st using larger needles
Check your tension before beginning.

Note
Read chart from right to left for RS knit rows and left to right for WS purl rows.
Main colour fleck yarn is knitted double throughout. To knit the white garment, use a medium weight cotton knitted singly.
Work each rose motif with separate balls of yarn and weave in main colour loosely across back of work (see page 114).

■ BACK
Using smaller needles and A, cast on 69[71:75] sts and work in rib as foll:
1st rib row (RS) K1, *P1, K1, rep from * to end.
2nd rib row P1, *K1, P1, rep from * to end.
Rep last 2 rows until rib measures 8cm, ending with a first row.
Inc row Rib 3[1:3], (M1, rib 3) 4[2:1] times, (M1, rib 2) 21[29:33] times, (M1, rib 3) 4[2:1] times. 98[104:110] sts.
Change to larger needles and st st and work in patt from row 1 of body chart for 54 rows.

Armhole shaping
Dec one st at each end of next and every foll alternate row to end of row 126[130:134]. 26[28:30] sts.
Cast off.

■ FRONT
Work as for back to end of row 114 [114:116], but do not work top flower motif. 38[44:50] sts.

Neck shaping
Next row K2tog, patt 10[13:16] sts, turn and leave rem sts on a spare needle.
Work one row.
Dec one st at each end of next and every alternate row to 3[2:3] sts.
Work one row.
2nd size:
K2tog and fasten off.

First and 3rd sizes:
Sl 1, K2tog, psso, fasten off.
With RS facing rejoin A to rem sts, cast off centre 14 sts and work to match first side, reversing all shapings.

■ SLEEVES (Make 2)
Using smaller needles and A, cast on 33[37:41] sts and work in rib as for back for 8cm, ending with a first row.
Inc row Rib 3, (M1, rib 2) 15[17:19] times. 48[54:60] sts.
Change to larger needles and work in patt from row 1 of sleeve chart, inc one st at each end of 3rd and every foll alternate row to 72[78:84] sts.
Work one row. (row 26)
Inc one st at each end of next and every foll 3rd row to 96[102:108] sts.
Work 6 rows without shaping.
Dec one st at each end of next (row 67) and every foll alternate row 10 times. 76[82:88] sts. (row 85)
Dec one st at each end of next 2 rows.
Next row Patt to end.

All measurements are in centimetres.

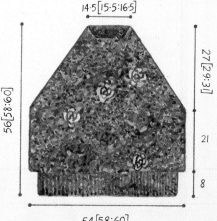

14·5[15·5:16·5]
27[29:31]
21
8
56[58:60]
54[58:60]
FRONT/BACK

53[57:60]
2[3:4]
26[27:29]
25
8
59[60:62]
27[30:33]
SLEEVE

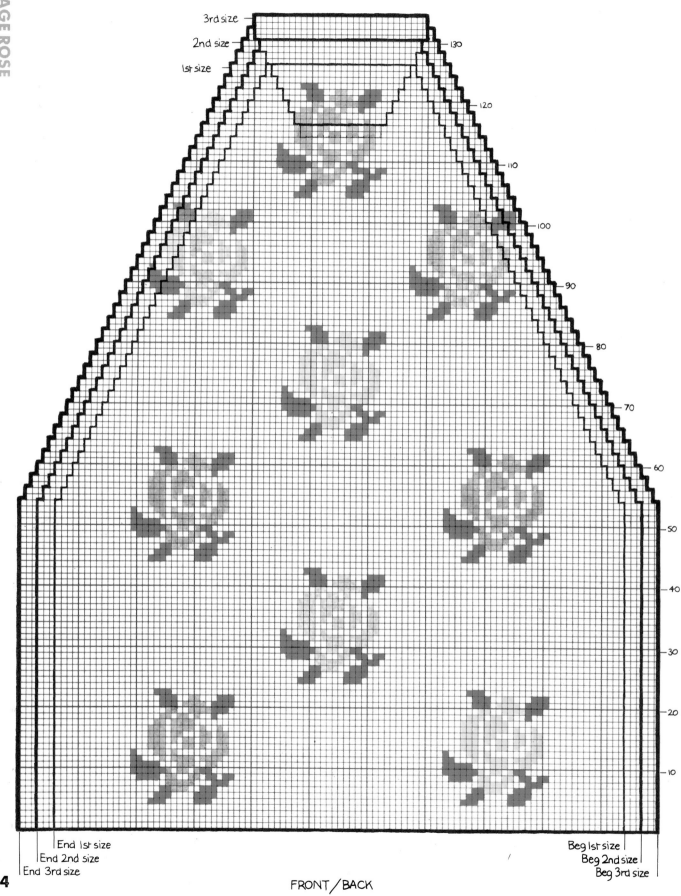

3rd size
2nd size
1st size

130

120

110

100

90

80

70

60

50

40

30

20

10

End 1st size
End 2nd size
End 3rd size

Beg 1st size
Beg 2nd size
Beg 3rd size

44

FRONT / BACK

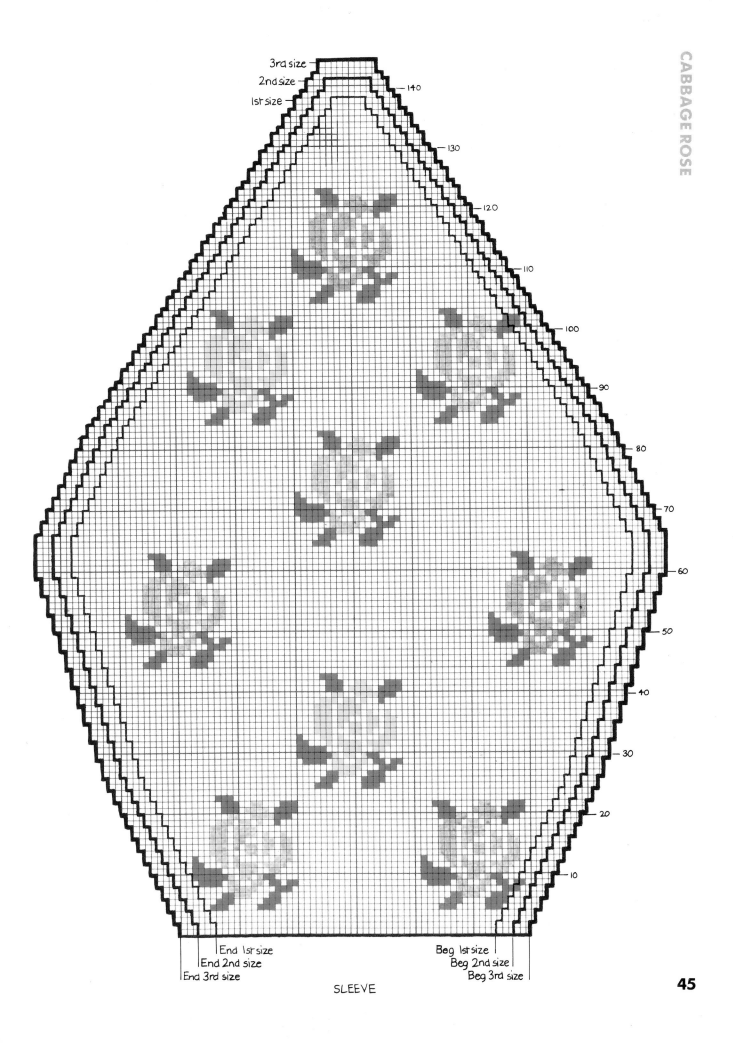

3rd size —

2nd size — — 140

1st size —

— 130

— 120

— 110

— 100

— 90

— 80

— 70

— 60

— 50

— 40

— 30

— 20

— 10

End 1st size — Beg 1st size
End 2nd size — Beg 2nd size
End 3rd size — Beg 3rd size

SLEEVE

45

Rep last 3 rows to 6[8:10] sts.
Cast off.

■ MAKING UP
Raglan ribs (Make 4)
These are worked along shaped
edges of top of raglan sleeves. With RS
facing and using smaller needles and
A, pick up and K61 sts evenly along
shaped edge and work in rib as for
back for 4cm.
Cast off loosely in rib.

Join sleeve edges to armhole edges,
leave left back open.

Neckband
With RS facing and using smaller
needles and A, pick up and K4 sts
along raglan rib, 6[8:10] sts across top
of sleeve, 4 sts along raglan rib,
29[35:39] sts around front neck, 4 sts
along raglan rib, 6[8:10] sts at top of
sleeve, 4 sts along raglan rib,
24[26:28] sts across back neck.
81[93:103] sts.
Work in rib as for back for 8cm.
Cast off loosely in rib.
Sew in ends and press pieces on
WS under damp cloth or with
steam iron.
Join rem raglan sleeve and collar
edge. (Join collar on RS.)
Join side and sleeve seams.
Fold neckband in half to outside and
stitch down carefully.

SUGARED ALMOND

JANICE WILKINS

The muted pastel tones used soften the rectangular shapes in this stylish shawl-collared sweater. The blocks are worked in stocking stitch and eyelet stitch.

■ SIZE
To fit 81-86[91-97]cm/32-34[36-38]in bust
Figures for larger sizes are given in square brackets. Where there is only one set of figures, this applies to both sizes.
See diagram for finished measurements.

■ MATERIALS
Use a medium weight cotton yarn.
260[280]g main colour A (white)
190[210]g 1st contrast B (green)
160[180]g 2nd contrast C (pale green)
190[210]g 3rd contrast D (orange)
One pair each of 3mm and 3¾mm knitting needles *or size to obtain correct tension*

■ TENSION
24 sts and 28 rows to 10cm over st st using larger needles
Check your tension before beginning.

Note
For ease of working, the collar may be made in 2 pieces and joined at centre back.

■ BACK
Using smaller needles, cast on 24[27] sts with A, 35[38] sts with D, 32[33] sts with C, 24[27] sts with B. 115[125] sts.
Keeping colours correct, work in rib as foll:
1st rib row (RS) K1, *P1, K1, rep from * to end.
2nd rib row P1, *K1, P1, rep from * to end.
Rep last 2 rows until rib measures 8cm, ending with a first row.
Inc row Rib 3, (M1, rib 6) 18[20] times, M1, rib to end. 134[146] sts.
Change to larger needles and beg patt as foll:
1st row (RS) K45[51]A, K27B, (K1A, K1D) 10 times, K42[48]C.
2nd row P42[48]C, (P1D, P1A) 10 times, P27B, P45[51]A.
3rd row K5A, (yfwd, K2togA, K4A) 6[7] times, yfwd, K2togA, K2A, K27B, (K1A, K1D) 10 times, K42[48]C.
4th row As 2nd row.
5th and 6th rows As first and 2nd rows.
7th row K2A, (yfwd, K2togA, K4A) 7[8] times, K1A, K27B, (K1A, K1D) 10 times, K42[48]C.
8th row As 2nd row.
Last 8 rows form patt for first strip of colour rectangles.
Cont in patt as set until 25[27] rows have been completed.

Beg 2nd strip of colour rectangles as foll:
1st row (WS) P37[43]B, P33A, P32D, (P1A, P1D) 16[19] times.
2nd row (K1D, K1A) 16[19] times, K32D, K33A, K5B, (yfwd, K2togB, K4B) 4[5] times, yfwd, K2togB, K6B.
3rd row As first row.
4th row (K1D, K1A) 16[19] times, K32D, K33A, K37[43]B.
5th row As first row.
6th row (K1D, K1A) 16[19] times, K32D, K33A, K2B, (yfwd, K2togB, K4B) 5[6] times, yfwd, K2togB, K3B.
7th row As first row.
8th row As 4th row.
Last 8 rows form patt for 2nd strip of colour rectangles.
Cont in patt as set until 25[27] rows of this strip have been completed.
Beg 3rd strip of colour rectangles as foll:
1st row (RS) K42[48]B, K32C, (K1B, K1D) 15 times, K30[36]A.
2nd row P30[36]A, (P1D, P1B) 15 times, P32C, P42[48]B.
3rd row K42[48]B, K5C,(yfwd, K2togC, K4C) 4 times, yfwd, K2togC, K1C, (K1B, K1D) 15 times, K30[36]A.
4th row As 2nd row.
5th and 6th rows As first and 2nd rows.
7th row K42[48]B, K2C, (yfwd, K2togC, K4C) 5 times, (K1B, K1D) 15 times, K30[36]A.
8th row As 2nd row.
Last 8 rows form patt for 3rd strip of colour rectangles.
Cont in patt as set until 25[27] rows have been completed, placing a marker at both ends of 23rd[25th] row.
Beg 4th strip of colour rectangles as foll:

1st row (WS) P42[48]C, P35D, (P1B, P1C) 12 times, P33[39]A.
2nd row K33[39]A, (K1C, K1B) 12 times, K35D, K5C, (yfwd, K2togC, K4C) 6[7] times, K1C.
3rd row As first row.
4th row K33[39]A, (K1C, K1B) 12 times, K35D, K42[48]C.
5th row As first row.
6th row K33[39]A, (K1C, K1B) 12 times, K35D, K2C, (yfwd, K2togC, K4C) 6[7] times, yfwd, K2togC, K3C.
7th row As first row.
8th row As 4th row.
Last 8 rows form patt for 4th strip of colour rectangles.
Cont in patt as set until 25[27] rows have been completed.
Beg 5th strip of colour rectangles as foll:
1st row (RS) K27[33]D, K36C, K25A, (K1D, K1A) 23[26] times.
2nd row (P1A, P1D) 23[26] times, P25A, P36C, P27[33]D.
3rd row K27[33]D, K5C, (yfwd, K2togC,K4C) 5 times, K1C, K25A, (K1D, K1A) 23[26] times.
4th row As 2nd row.
5th and 6th rows As first and 2nd rows.
7th row K27[33]D, K2C, (yfwd, K2togC, K4C) 5 times, yfwd, K2togC, K2C, K25A, (K1D, K1A) 23[26] times.
8th row As 2nd row.
Last 8 rows form patt for 5th strip of colour rectangles.
Cont in patt as set until 25[27] rows have been completed.
Beg 6th strip of colour rectangles as foll:

By replacing the four pastel colours with a monochromatic scheme, the brick-like build up of rectangles on this design produces a more austere and striking garment.

1st row (WS) P18[24]B, P44D, (P1A, P1B) 14 times, P44[50]A.
2nd row K44[50]A, (K1B, K1A) 14 times, K5D, (yfwd, K2togD, K4D) 6 times, yfwd, K2togD, K1D, K18[24]B.
3rd row As first row.
4th row K44[50]A, (K1D, K1A) 14 times, K32D, K44D, K18[24]B.
5th row As first row.
6th row K44[50]A, (K1D, K1A) 14 times, K2D, (yfwd, K2togD, K4D) 7 times, K18[24]B.
7th row As first row.
8th row As 4th row.
Last 8 rows form patt for 6th strip of colour rectangles.
Cont in patt as set until 25[29] rows have been completed.
Cast off.

■ FRONT

Work as for back until 70[76] rows of patt have been worked.

Neck shaping
Next row Patt 66[72] sts, turn and leave rem sts on a spare needle.
Work 2 rows.
Place a marker at both ends of last row.
Dec one st at neck edge on next and every foll 3rd row until 45[51] sts rem.
Cont without shaping until front

measures same as back to shoulder.
Cast off.
With RS facing, rejoin yarn to rem sts, cast off 2 sts, patt to end.
Work to match first side, reversing shaping.

■ SLEEVES (Make 2)

Using smaller needles, cast on 24 sts with D and 21 sts with C. 45 sts.
Work in rib as for back for 7cm.
Inc row Rib 3, (M1, rib 3) 13 times, rib 3. 58 sts.
Change to larger needles and beg patt as foll:
1st row (RS) K7A, K27B, (K1A, K1D) 10 times, K4C.

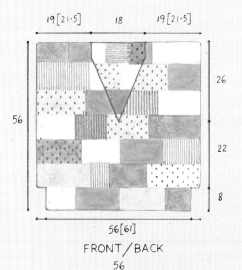

19[21·5]   18   19[21·5]

56

56[61]

FRONT / BACK

26

22

8

FRONT / BACK

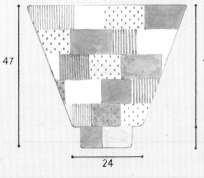

56

47

40

7

24

SLEEVE

Last row sets position of strips as for centre 58 sts of back.
Cont in patt as set for back, inc one st at each end of 3rd and every foll 3rd row until there are 134 sts.
Cont in patt without shaping until sleeve measures 47cm.
Cast off.

■ COLLAR

Using larger needles and A, cast on 242 sts and using A and B work in st st and 2 colour stripe patt for 26 rows.
Using A only, work 4 rows more.
Cast off.

■ MAKING UP

Press according to instructions on yarn label.
Join shoulder seams.
Sew cast off edge of sleeve between markers on back and front.
Join side and sleeve seams.
Turn plain edge of collar to WS and sew to form hem.
Sew collar evenly to neck edge.

RACING COLOURS

Vivid streaks of colour bring this black and green checked slipover to life. The garment has deep armholes and is designed to be worn over another top. You could catch stitch the armholes to reduce the depth.

■ SIZE

To fit 86-91[97-102]cm/34-36[38-40]in bust
Figures for larger sizes are given in square brackets. Where there is only one set of figures, this applies to all sizes.
See diagram for finished measurements.

■ MATERIALS

Use a medium weight cotton yarn.
350[400]g main colour A (black)
250g 1st contrast B (olive green)
50g each in 3 contrast colours C, D, E (yellow, orange, pale blue)
One pair of 4mm knitting needles
One 4½mm circular knitting needle 30cm long
One 4½mm circular knitting needle 60cm long *or size to obtain correct tension*

The darts of colour make a bold statement across this slipover tabard. This variation has an off-beat background check of orange and brown with a beautiful bright focus in the turquoise, yellow and lime green.

■ TENSION

20 sts and 22 rows to 10cm over check patt using larger needles
Check your tension before beginning.

Note

When working check patt, carry colour not in use loosely across back of work (see page 114).
Back and front are each worked back and forth in rows on a circular needle so that two RS rows or two WS rows can be worked one after another by slipping sts to other end of needle and working back across them in the same direction as the last row.

■ BACK

** Using A and smaller needles, cast on 104[108] sts and work in rib as foll:
1st rib row *K4, P4, rep from * to end.
Rep last row 9 times.
Change to longer circular needle and beg check patt, working back and forth in rows as foll:
1st row (RS) *K2 in A, K2 in B, rep from * to end.
2nd row *P2 in B, P2 in A, rep from * to end.
3rd and 4th rows As first and 2nd rows.
5th row *K2 in B, K2 in A, rep from * to end.
6th row *P2 in A, P2 in B, rep from * to end.
7th and 8th rows As 5th and 6th rows.
These 8 rows form check patt.
Beg first short stripe as foll:
9th row Using C only, K44 sts, turn and leave rem sts unworked.
10th row Sl 1, P to end
11th row K42, turn.
12th row As 10th row.
13th row K40, turn.

14th row As 10th row.
15th to 22nd rows As first to 8th rows.
23rd row Slip all sts to other end of needle and with WS facing and using D only, P44 sts, turn and leave rem sts unworked.
24th row Sl 1, K to end.
25th row P42, turn.
26th row As 24th row.
27th row P40, turn.
28th row As 24th row.
29th to 36th rows Slip all sts to other end of needle and beg with RS facing, work as for first to 8th rows.
37th row Slip first 30[34] sts onto RH needle, using E, K44, turn.
38th row Sl 1, P42, turn.
39th row Sl 1, K40, turn.
40th row Sl 1, P38, turn.
41st row Sl 1, K36, turn.
42nd row Sl 1, P34, turn.
Rep these 42 rows twice *and at the same time* inc 2 sts at beg of first and 2nd rows only (108[116] sts) and work 2 extra sts in C and D stripes and slip 2 extra sts onto RH needle on row 37.**
Cont without shaping in check patt only, work 20[24] rows.

Neck shaping

Next row Work first 34[38] sts in check patt, turn and leave rem sts on a spare needle.
Cont without shaping for 9 rows.
Cast off.
With RS facing, slip centre 40 sts onto st holder for back neck and rejoin yarns to rem 34[38] sts and work to match first side.

■ FRONT

Work as back from ** to **, but working C stripes on left side of work and D stripes on right side of work, so that short stripes match at side seams.
Cont without shaping in check patt only, work 12[16] rows.

Neck shaping

Next row Work first 34[38] sts in check patt, turn and leave rem sts on a spare needle.
Cont without shaping, work 17 rows.
Cast off.
With RS facing, slip centre 40 sts onto st holder for front neck and rejoin yarns to rem 34[38] sts and work to match first side.

■ NECKBAND

Join shoulder seams.
With RS facing and using shorter circular needle, work in check patt across 40 sts of centre back from st holder, pick up and patt 16 sts evenly down left side of neck, patt across 40 sts of front neck from st holder, pick up and patt 16 sts evenly up right side of neck. 112 sts.
Work 15 rounds in check patt.
Cast off.

All measurements are in centimetres.

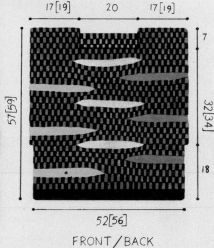

17[19] 20 17[19]

57[59]

7

32[34]

18

52[56]

FRONT/BACK

■ ARMBANDS
Join side seams.
With RS facing and using longer
circular needle, pick up and K152[156]
sts around armhole and work 12
rounds in K2, P2 rib.
Cast off.

■ MAKING UP
Press according to instructions on yarn
label.

WAVEBAND

This generously proportioned
T-shaped top flatters any figure.
Knitted in black and lurex yarn, it would
make a sophisticated evening top.

■ SIZE
One size to fit up to 107cm/42in bust
*See diagram for finished
measurements.*

■ MATERIALS
Use a lightweight cotton yarn.
650g main colour A (white)
50g contrast B (black)
50g contrast C (orange)
One pair each of 3¼mm and 3¾mm
knitting needles *or size to obtain
correct tension*

■ TENSION
23 sts and 28 rows to 10cm over st st
using larger needles
Check your tension before beginning.

Note
Read chart from right to left for RS knit
rows and left to right for WS purl rows.
Unless stated st st is used throughout.
Do not carry contrast yarn across back
of work (see page 114).

■ BACK AND FRONT (Both alike)
Using smaller needles and A, cast on
139 sts and work in rib as foll:
1st rib row (RS) K1, *P1, K1, rep from *
to end.
2nd rib row P1, *K1, P1, rep from * to
end.
Rep last 2 rib rows twice, inc one st in
last row. 140 sts.
Change to larger needles and work
without shaping from row 1 of chart to
end of row 98.
Mark both ends of last row for
armholes.
Cont without shaping to end of row
168.

Neck shaping
Next row Patt 47 sts, turn and leave
rem sts on a spare needle.
Cast off 4 sts at beg of next row.
Work one row.
Cast off 3 sts at beg of next row.
Dec one st at neck edge on next 5
rows. 35 sts.
Cont without shaping to end of chart.
Cast off.
With RS facing, rejoin yarn to rem sts,
cast off centre 46 sts, patt to end.
Work to match first side, reversing
shaping.

■ FIRST SLEEVE
Using smaller needles, cast on 115 sts
and work in rib as for back. 116 sts.
Change to larger needles and work in
patt from row 1 of sleeve chart,

shaping sides by inc one st at each end
of every 3rd row until there are 138 sts.
Cont without shaping to end of chart.
Cast off.

■ SECOND SLEEVE
Work as for first sleeve, working first
stripe in B and 2nd stripe in C.

■ NECKBAND
Join right shoulder.
With RS facing and using larger
needles and A, pick up and K63 sts
evenly around front neck and 63 sts
evenly around back neck. 126 sts.
Beg with a P row, work in st st for 13
rows.
Cast off.

■ MAKING UP
Press according to instructions on yarn
label.
Join left shoulder and neckband.
Sew cast off edge of sleeves to back
and front between markers.
Join side and sleeve seams.

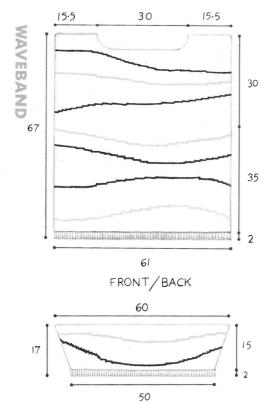

WAVEBAND

15·5 30 15·5

67

30

35

2

61

FRONT / BACK

60

17 15

2

50

SLEEVE

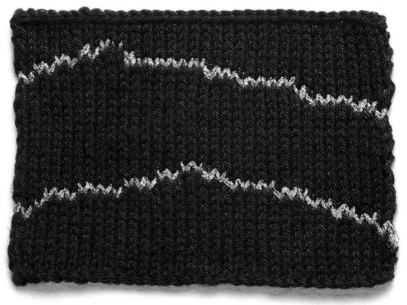

Black cotton yarn and a double strand of lurex change this big T-shirt to a sophisticated evening alternative.

All measurements are in centimetres.

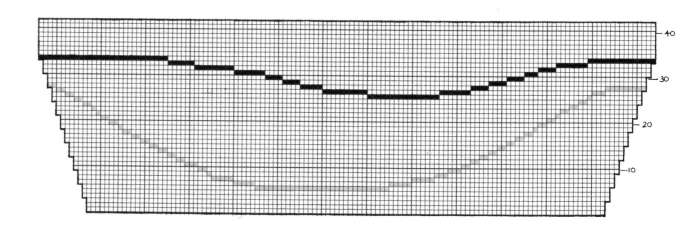

40

30

20

10

FIRST SLEEVE

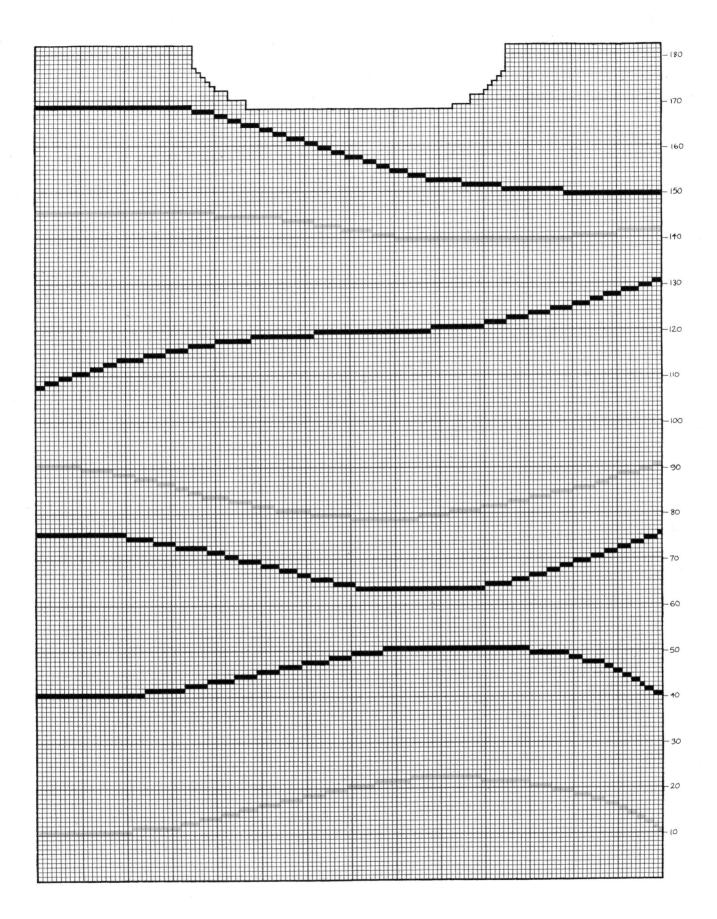

FRONT/BACK

55

RAZZLE DAZZLE

Multi-coloured triangles and spots combine in this easy-to-knit summer top. The mixture of garter and stocking stitch adds texture to a vibrant but simple garment. The shanked buttons are purely decorative.

■ SIZE
To fit 81-86[91-97]cm/32-34[36-38]in bust
Figures for larger sizes are given in square brackets. Where there is only one set of figures, this applies to all sizes.
See diagram for finished measurements.

■ MATERIALS
Use a fine mercerised cotton yarn.
250[300]g main colour A (pink)
50[50]g 1st contrast B (turquoise)
50[50]g 2nd contrast C (blue)
One pair each of 3mm and 3¼mm knitting needles *or size to obtain correct tension*
Eight 20mm buttons

■ TENSION
24 sts and 46 rows to 10cm over garter st using larger needles
Check your tension before beginning.

Note
Read chart from right to left for RS odd numbered rows and left to right for WS even numbered rows.
Use separate ball of yarn for each spot (see page 114).

■ FRONT AND BACK (Both alike)
Triangles
Using larger needles and A, cast on 2 sts.
1st row K2.
2nd row Beg row with yarn at front of work and over right hand needle to make a loop – called yo –, K2.
3rd row Yo, K3.
4th row Yo, K4.
Cont in this way until end of row 13. 14 sts. This completes first triangle.
Make 6 more triangles using C for the next triangle, then A, B, A, C, A and beg each triangle by casting the 2 sts onto the free needle. *Do not break yarn at end of last point.*
Using A only, K across all 98 sts.
1st size only:
Knit 9 rows.
2nd size only:
Knit next 4 rows, working a yo at beg of each row. 102 sts.
Knit one row more.
Both sizes:
Cont without shaping from row 11 of chart, working background in g st and spots in st st.
Foll chart until 148th row has been

completed. Knit 8 rows. Front should measure approx 34cm from top of triangles.
Change to smaller needles and using A only, work 10 rows in K1, P1 rib. Cast off loosely in rib.

■ STRAPS (Make 4)
Using B, cast on 2 sts.
1st row K2.
2nd row Yo, K2.
3rd row Yo, K3.
4th row Yo, K4.
5th row Yo, K5.
6th row Yo, K6.
7th row Yo, K7. 8 sts.
Knit 4 rows without shaping.
Next row K1, P1, K4, P1, K1.
Next row P.
Rep last 2 rows 64 times, or until strap measures desired length.
Knit 4 rows.
K2tog at beg of next and every foll row until 2 sts rem.
Cast off.
Make one more strap in B and 2 straps in C.

■ MAKING UP
Press gently according to instructions on yarn label, but avoid stretching while pressing. Join side seams.

Overlapping strap on front by approx 5cm, sew one strap in B and one strap in C to each side, placing first strap of each pair 6cm from side seam and 2nd strap 11cm from side seam. Cross each pair of straps approx 12cm from each end and sew tog at crossings. Sew straps to back in the same way as for front. Sew one button to each strap end.

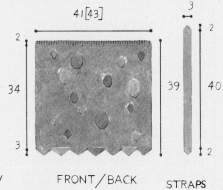

FRONT/BACK   STRAPS

All measurements are in centimetres.

The background colour and the contrasts have been changed around on this alternative version.

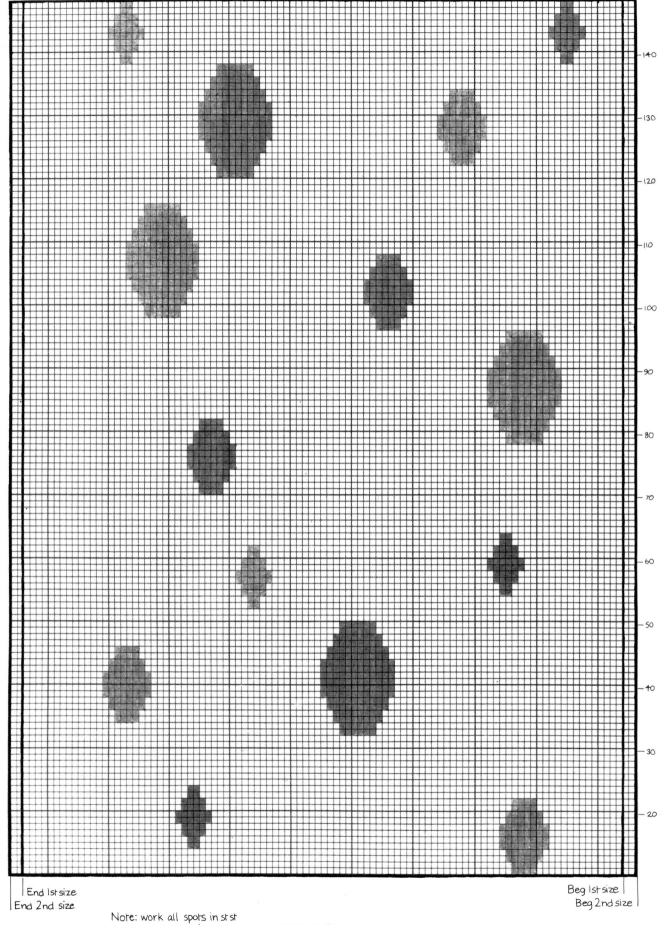

End 1st size
End 2nd size

Beg 1st size
Beg 2nd size

Note: work all spots in st st
and background in garter st   FRONT/BACK

CHEQUERBOARD

Horizontal and vertical stripes in a monochromatic scheme make a clear visual impact on this traditional cardigan shape. The garment is worked in one piece to the armholes.

■ SIZE

To fit 86[91:97-102]cm/34[36:38-40]in bust
Figures for larger sizes are given in square brackets. Where there is only one set of figures, this applies to all sizes.
See diagram for finished measurements.

■ MATERIALS

Use a lightweight cotton yarn.
200[220:250]g each in contrast A (black) and B (white)
150g each in contrast C (medium grey) and D (slate grey)
150g contrast E (light grey)
One each of 3¼mm and 3¾mm circular knitting needle 60cm long *or size to obtain correct tension*
Eight 14mm buttons

■ TENSION

24 sts and 30 rows to 10cm over block patt using larger needle
Check your tension before beginning.

Note

When working with two colours in a row, weave colour not in use loosely across back of work (see page 114). Garment is worked in one piece to armholes.

■ BODY

Using smaller needle and A, cast on 226[246:254] sts and working back and forth in rows on circular needle, beg rib as foll:
1st rib row (RS) *P2 in A, K2 in B, rep from * ending with P2 in A.
2nd rib row *K2 in A, P2 in B, rep from * ending with K2 in A.
Rep last 2 rows until rib measures 8cm, ending with a WS row.
Change to larger needle and knit 2 rows in C, dec one st in middle of first row for first and 2nd sizes and inc one st in middle of first row for 3rd size. 225[245:255] sts.
Beg block patt as foll:
Next row (RS) Foll row 3 of chart 1 from right to left, K across row beg and ending as indicated on chart.
Cont foll chart, working first 3rd-7th rows of chart in st st, foll by 2 purl rows in E to form ridge.
Cont in patt in this way (foll chart and always working ridge into 2 stripe rows) without shaping until 63rd row of chart is complete and body measures approx 29cm from beg.

Armhole shaping

Slip 55[60:63] sts from each side of work onto a st holder for fronts and cont on centre 115[125:129] sts for back.

■ BACK YOKE

Using A and beg with a RS row, knit 2 rows, casting off 15[18:19] sts at beg of each row. 85[89:91] sts.
Beg with row 66 of chart 2 for yoke, work in patt without shaping foll chart and working ridged stripes as before, until 124th[126th:128th] row of chart is complete and armhole measures approx 20[21:22]cm.
Slip sts onto a st holder.

■ RIGHT FRONT YOKE

Slip sts of right front onto larger needle and beg with a RS, knit 2 rows, casting off 15[18:19] sts at beg of 2nd row. 40[42:44] sts.
Beg with row 66 of chart 2 for yoke, work in patt as for back yoke without shaping until armhole measures 16[17:18]cm, ending with a WS row.

Neck shaping

Cont in patt, casting off 8[9:10] sts at beg of next row (neck edge), then dec one st at neck edge on every row 11 times. 21[22:23] sts.
Cont in patt without shaping until there are the same number of rows as back to shoulder.

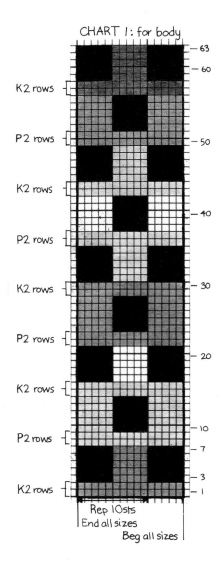

CHART 1: for body

K2 rows
P2 rows
K2 rows
P2 rows
K2 rows
P2 rows
K2 rows
P2 rows
K2 rows

— 63
— 60
— 50
— 40
— 30
— 20
— 10
— 7
— 3
— 1

Rep 10 sts
End all sizes
Beg all sizes

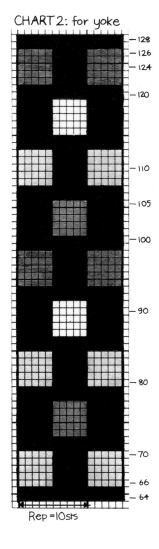

CHART 2: for yoke

— 128
— 126
— 124
— 120
— 110
— 105
— 100
— 90
— 80
— 70
— 66
— 64

Rep = 10 sts

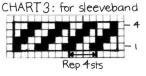

CHART 3: for sleeveband

— 4
— 1

Rep 4 sts

Shoulder shaping
** Beg with a WS row and using A, purl 2 rows, knit one row, purl one row. Using E, purl one row. Knit one row.**
Rep from ** to ** twice more.
Using A, purl 2 rows. knit one row. Cast off these shoulder sts with sts of right back shoulder by placing WS of back and front tog and casting off first st of back shoulder with first st of front shoulder and so on to form a ridge on the RS.

■ LEFT FRONT YOKE
Work left front yoke as for right front yoke reversing shaping.

■ SLEEVES (Make 2)
Sleeves are worked directly onto body of sweater by picking up sts around armholes.
With RS facing and using larger needle and B, pick up and K115[120:125] sts evenly along armhole edge, omitting cast off edge at underarm.
Still using B and working back and forth in rows, knit one row.
*** Using A, knit 2 rows, purl one row, knit one row.
Work next 4 rows in st st, foll chart 3 for sleeve band. ***
Rep from *** to *** twice more.
Using A, knit 2 rows, purl one row, knit one row.
Work in patt foll charts, beg with 105th row of chart 2 and working backwards to 64th row, then cont on chart 1, beg with 63rd row and working backwards to first row *and at the same time* shape sleeve by dec one st at each end of 6th row once and then every 4th row 24 times. 65[70:75] sts.
Then on last row of patt (row 1 of chart 1) dec 9[14:19] sts evenly across row. 56 sts.
Change to smaller needle and work in rib as for welt for 5cm.
Cast off in A.

■ NECKBAND
With RS facing and using smaller needle and A, beg at right front neck and pick up and K40[41:42] sts along right side of neck, K43[45:47] sts from back neck holder dec one st at centre back, pick up and K40[42:44] sts along left side of neck. 122[126:130] sts.

Working back and forth in rows, knit one row in A.
Work in rib as for welt for 8 rows.
Cast off firmly in A.

■ BUTTONHOLE BAND
With RS facing and using smaller needle and A, pick up and K108[110:112] sts along right front including neckband.
Work 2 rows in rib as for welt.
Next row Rib 4[4,2], cast off 2 sts, *rib 12[12:13], cast off 2 sts, rep from * to last 4[6:3] sts, rib 2[4:4].
Next row Rib, casting on 2 sts over those cast off in last row.
Work 2 rows in rib. Cast off in A.

■ BUTTONBAND
Work as for buttonhole band, omitting buttonholes.

■ MAKING UP
Press lightly on WS with a warm iron.
Join sleeve seam matching patts and sewing first part of top of sleeve to cast off sts at underarm.
Darn in all loose ends.
Sew on buttons opposite buttonholes.

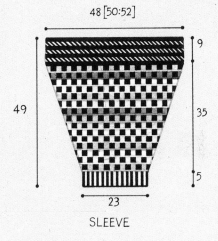

48 [50:52]

9

49

35

5

23

SLEEVE

All measurements are in centimetres.

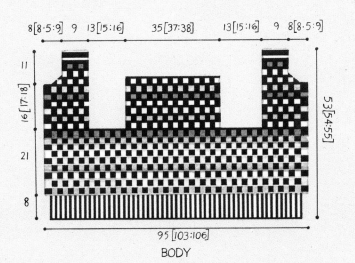

8[8·5:9] 9 13[15:16] 35[37:38] 13[15:16] 9 8[8·5:9]

11

16[17:18]

21

8

53[54:55]

95 [103:106]

BODY

FIESTA

An off-the-shoulder design is ideal for hot sunny days or for evening wear. The scoop neck frill in this green flecked top is knitted onto a simple shape and pulled tight to fit with a drawstring.

■ SIZE

To fit 86[91:97-102]cm/34[36:38-40]in bust
Figures for larger sizes are given in square brackets. Where there is only one set of figures, this applies to all sizes.
See diagram for finished measurements.

■ MATERIALS

300[300:325]g fine cotton yarn
One pair each of 3¼mm and 4mm knitting needles *or size to obtain correct tension*
One 2.50mm crochet hook

■ TENSION

23 sts and 26 rows to 10cm over st st using larger needles
Check your tension before beginning.

■ BACK AND FRONT (Both alike)

Using smaller needles, cast on 85 sts and work in rib as foll:
1st rib row (RS) K1, *P1, K1, rep from * to end.
2nd rib row P1, *K1, P1, rep from * to end.
Rep last 2 rows until rib measures 6cm, ending with a WS row.
Change to larger needles and beg with a K row, work in st st shaping sides by inc one st at each end of 5th and every foll 6th row until there are 97[101:109] sts.
Cont without shaping until work measures 46[47:48]cm.
Cast off.

■ FRILL (Back and front alike)

Using larger needles, cast on 15 sts.
1st and every foll alternate row K2, P to last st, K1.
2nd row (RS) K9, yfwd, sl 1, K1, psso, yfwd, K4.
4th row K8, (yfwd, sl 1, K1, psso) twice, yfwd, K4.
6th row K7, (yfwd, sl 1, K1, psso) 3 times, yfwd, K4.
8th row K6, (yfwd, sl 1, K1, psso) 4 times, yfwd, K4.
10th row K5, (yfwd, sl 1, K1, psso) 5 times, yfwd, K4.
12th row K4, (yfwd, sl 1, K1, psso) 6 times, yfwd, K4.
14th row K5, (yfwd, sl 1, K1, psso) 6 times, K2tog, K2.
16th row K6, (yfwd, sl 1, K1, psso) 5 times, K2tog, K2.
18th row K7, (yfwd, sl 1, K1, psso) 4 times, K2tog, K2..
20th row K8, (yfwd, sl 1, K1, psso) 3 times, K2tog, K2.
22nd row K9, (yfwd, sl 1, K1, psso) twice, K2tog, K2.
24th row K10, yfwd, sl 1, K1, psso, K2tog, K2.
These 24 rows form patt.
Work 11 patt reps more.
Cast off.

■ TOP EDGING

Thread a sharp needle with a length of yarn and make a running stitch along top edge of both frills. With RS facing, place along top edge of body, gather evenly to fit body leaving two complete frill patts either side for shoulder straps. Tack in place.
With RS facing and using smaller needles, pick up and K147[151:159] sts evenly along top, through frill and body, thus attaching frill to body.
Work 2 rows in K1, P1 rib.
Eyelet row Rib 2, *rib 2tog, yfwd, rib 1, rep from * to last 1[2:1] sts, rib to end.
Work 2 rows more in rib.
Cast off.

■ MAKING UP

Press according to instructions on yarn label.
Join side seams leaving top 13cm open for armhole and join frill seams.
Edge armhole with one row of double crochet.
Make a 2m long plait or twist of yarn, knot approx 3cm from each end for tassels.
Thread through eyelets and tie in a bow at front.

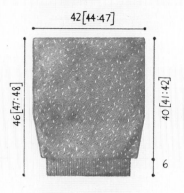

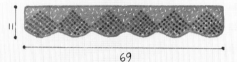

FRONT / BACK

FRILL

11

69

All measurements are in centimetres.

42[44:47]

46[47:48]

40[41:42]

6

RIPPLES

This clever alternating of neutral striped panels in both sweater and jacket looks complicated to knit, but it is not. Each section is knitted onto the previous section, and there is the minimum of making up at the finish. A variation on the pattern, turning it into a jacket, is given overleaf.

■ SIZE
One size to fit up to 97cm/38in bust
See diagram for finished measurements.

■ MATERIALS
1200g medium weight cotton yarn for sweater
100 g of contrast yarn for jacket version
One pair of 5mm knitting needles *or size to obtain correct tension*

■ TENSION
16 sts and 23 rows to 10cm over pattern
Check your tension before beginning.

■ STITCHES
1st and 3rd rows P.
2nd and 4th rows K.
5th and 7th rows K.
6th and 8th rows P.
These 8 rows form patt and are worked throughout.

Note
For the jacket version, work in 4 rows of contrast yarn at random on each section or following the photograph. Where chart details dec 2 sts at end of row, work 3 sts tog.

■ BACK
(Worked in 4 sections)
Section One
Cast on 50 sts and work in patt foll shaping from chart 1 for 102 rows.
Fasten off.
Section Two
With RS facing, pick up and K87 sts evenly along shaped edge of section one (A) and work in patt foll shaping from chart 2 for 96 rows, placing marker at beg of row 48.
Fasten off.
Section Three
With RS facing, pick up and K48 sts evenly along edge of section two from centre marker to left hand edge (B) and work in patt foll shaping from chart 3 for 69 rows.
Cast off rem 2 sts.
Section Four
With RS facing, pick up and K42 sts evenly along inside edge row ends of section three (C) and work in patt foll shaping from chart 4 for 86 rows.
Cast off rem 3 sts.

■ FRONT
(Worked in 4 sections)
Work first three sections as for back.
Section Four
Cast on one st and work in patt foll shaping from chart 4 for 86 rows.
Cast off rem 3 sts.

■ SLEEVES (Make 2)
(Worked in 2 sections)
Section One
Cast on 58 sts and work in patt foll shapings from chart 5 for 87 rows.
Cast off rem 24 sts.
Section Two
With RS facing, pick up and K61 sts evenly along straight edge of section one (D) and work in patt foll shaping from chart 6 for 69 rows.
Fasten off.

■ WELTS (Both alike)
With RS facing, pick up and K60 sts evenly along bottom edge.
Work in patt for 4 rows.
Cast off loosely.

■ CUFFS (Both alike)
With RS facing, pick up and K32 sts evenly along bottom sleeve edge.
Work in patt for 4 rows.
Cast off loosely.

■ COLLAR
Cast on 104 sts and work in patt for 32 rows.
Cast off loosely.

MAKING UP

Press according to instructions on yarn label.
Join section four to section two on front and back.
Join shoulder seams.
Sew sleeves to back and front.
Join side and sleeve seams.
Join short ends of collar and sew collar to neck edge.

JACKET

BACK

Work as for back of sweater.

SLEEVES

Work as for sleeves of sweater.

LEFT FRONT (Worked in 4 sections)

Section One
Cast on 50 sts and work in patt foll shaping from chart 7 for 102 rows.
Fasten off.

Section Two
With RS facing, pick up and K87 sts evenly along shaped edge of section one (A) and work in patt foll shaping from chart 8 for 60 rows, placing marker at beg of row 48.
Fasten off.

Section Three
With RS facing, pick up and K48 sts evenly along edge of section two from centre marker to left hand edge (B) and work in patt foll shaping from chart 9 for 69 rows.
Fasten off.

Section Four
With RS facing, pick up and K42 sts evenly along inside edge of row ends of section three (C) and work in patt foll shaping from chart 10 for 41 rows.
Fasten off.

RIGHT FRONT (Worked in 3 sections)

Section One
Cast on one st and work in patt foll shaping from chart 11 for 102 rows.
Fasten off.

Section Two
With RS facing, pick up and K51 sts evenly along shaped edge of section one (A) and work in patt foll shaping from chart 12 for 96 rows.
Fasten off.

Section Three
Cast on 2 sts and work in patt foll shaping from chart 13 for 55 rows.
52 sts.
56th row (WS) Patt 14 sts, turn and leave rem sts on a spare needle. Work rem rows on left hand side of chart.
Fasten off.
With WS facing, rejoin yarn to rem 38 sts, work 3sts tog, patt to end.
Work rem rows of right hand side of chart.
Fasten off.

BACK WELT

With RS facing, pick up and K60 sts evenly along bottom edge of back.
Work in patt for 12 rows.
Cast off.

FRONT WELTS (2 alike)

With RS facing, pick up and K30 sts evenly along bottom edge of both front sections.
Work in patt for 12 rows.
Cast off.

MAKING UP

Press according to instructions on yarn label.
Sew sleeves to back and fronts.
Join side and sleeve seams.

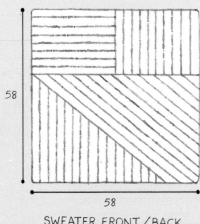

58

58

SWEATER FRONT/BACK
JACKET BACK

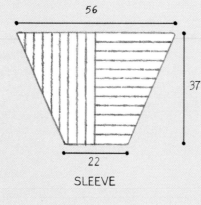

56

37

22

SLEEVE

All measurements are in centimetres.

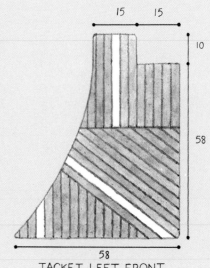

15   15

10

58

58

JACKET LEFT FRONT

SWEATER FRONT/BACK
JACKET BACK

1
SWEATER
FRONT/BACK
JACKET BACK

2
SWEATER
FRONT/BACK
JACKET BACK

3
SWEATER
FRONT/BACK
JACKET BACK

4
SWEATER
SWEATER BACK
SWEATER
FRONT

5
SWEATER/JACKET
SLEEVE

6
SWEATER/JACKET
SLEEVE

5   6

SWEATER/JACKET
SLEEVE

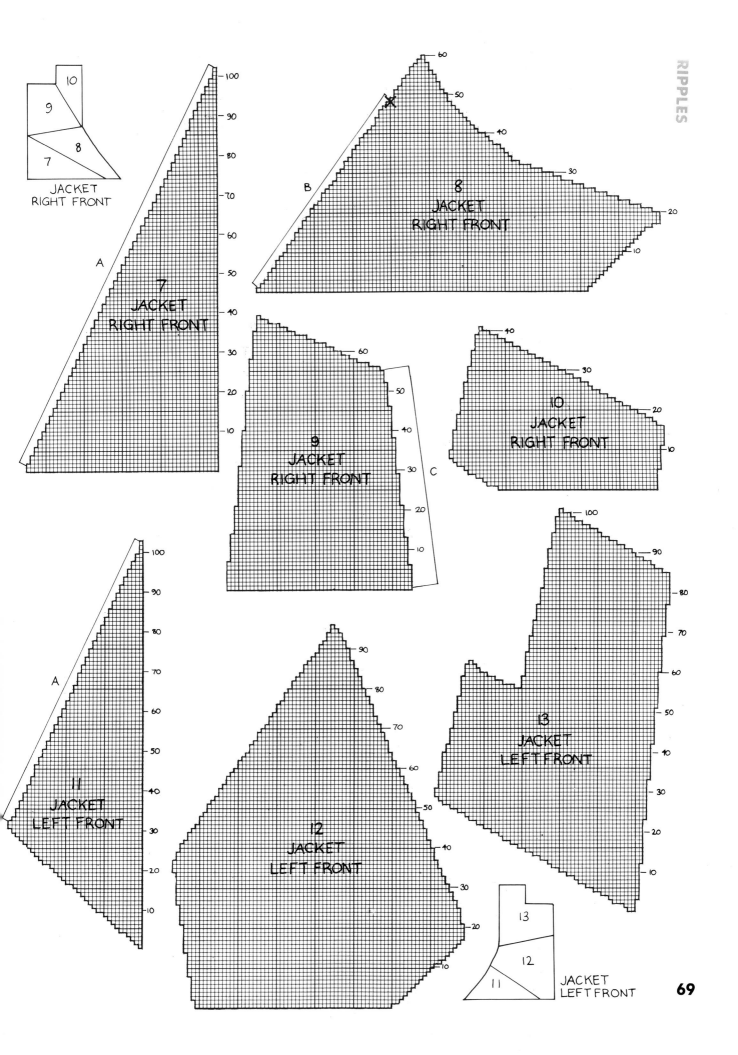

JACKET
RIGHT FRONT

7
JACKET
RIGHT FRONT

8
JACKET
RIGHT FRONT

9
JACKET
RIGHT FRONT

10
JACKET
RIGHT FRONT

11
JACKET
LEFT FRONT

12
JACKET
LEFT FRONT

13
JACKET
LEFT FRONT

JACKET
LEFT FRONT

STRIPE SURPRISE

By contrasting horizontal and vertical stripes in a simple colourway, this T-shaped sweater makes a dynamic impact. Experiment with stripes within this pattern to create your own unique combination (see page 73).

■ SIZE

To fit 81-86[91:97]cm/32-34[36:38]in bust
Figures for larger sizes are given in square brackets. Where there is only one set of figures, this applies to all sizes.
See diagram for finished measurements.

■ MATERIALS

Use a medium weight cotton yarn.
450[450:500]g main colour A (black)
300[300:350]g 1st contrast B (lilac)
100g 2nd contrast C (turquoise)
One pair of 4½mm knitting needles
One 4½mm circular knitting needle 30cm long
One 4½mm circular knitting needle 60cm long *or size to obtain correct tension*

■ TENSION

20 sts and 28 rows to 10cm over st st
Check your tension before beginning.

Note

Lower edge of sleeves and neckband are worked in st st and are meant to roll to RS.
Lower edge of back and front are worked in rev st st and are meant to roll to WS.

■ BACK

Using pair of needles and A, cast on 82[86:90] sts and beg with a K row, work in st st and stripe patt as foll:
* 20 rows using A.
10 rows using B. *
Rep from * to * without shaping until back measures 48[49:50]cm, ending with a WS row.

Neck shaping
Next row (RS) K25[26:27] sts, turn and leave rem sts on a spare needle.
Work 5 rows without shaping on these 25[26:27] sts.
Cast off.
With RS facing, slip centre 32[34:36] sts onto st holder for back neck.
Rejoin yarn to rem sts and work to match first side.

■ FRONT

Work as for back until front measures 43[44:45]cm, ending with a WS row.

Neck shaping
Next row (RS) K29[30:31] sts, leave rem sts on a spare needle.
Dec one st at beg of next and 3 foll alternate rows. 25[26:27] sts.
Work without shaping until front matches back to shoulder.
Cast off.
With RS facing, slip centre 24[26:28]sts onto st holder for front neck.
Rejoin yarn to rem sts and work to match first side, reversing shaping.

■ SLEEVES (Make 2)

Using pair of needles and A, cast on 40[44:46] sts and beg with a K row, work 4[8:12] rows in st st, inc one st at each end of last row. 42[46:48] sts.
Work 16[20:24] rows more in A, *and at the same time* shape sides by inc one st at each end of every 5th row.
Change to B and work in stripe patt as for back, beg with 10 rows B and cont to inc one st at each end of every 5th row until there are 84[88:92] sts.
Cont without shaping until sleeve measures approx 54[55:56]cm, ending with a stripe of 10 rows in B. Cast off.

■ UNDERARM INSETS (4 pieces)

Each underarm inset is made in 2 pieces — front and back.

Right front and left back inset
(Make 2)
Using pair of needles and A, cast on 80 sts.
1st row P to end.
2nd row Cast on 5 sts, K to end.
3rd row P50, (P2tog) twice, P to end.
4th row As 2nd row.
Using C, rep last 2 rows twice.
9th row Using A, as 3rd row.
Rows 2 to 9 form patt.

Cont in patt until 23 rows have been completed, ending with 3 rows in C. Cast off.

Right back and left front inset
(Make 2)
Using pair of needles and A, cast on 80 sts.
1st row K to end.
2nd row Cast on 5 sts, P to end.
3rd row K50, (K2tog) twice, K to end.

4th row As 2nd row.
Using C, rep last 2 rows twice.
9th row Using A, as 3rd row.
Rows 2 to 9 form patt.
Cont in patt until 23 rows have been completed, ending with 3 rows in C. Cast off.

■ **NECKBAND**
Join shoulder seams.
With RS facing and using shorter

circular needle and A, K across 32[34:36] sts of centre back from st holder, pick up and K18 sts evenly along left side of neck to centre front, K across 24[26:28] sts of centre front from st holder, pick up and K18 sts evenly along right side of neck. 92[96:100] sts.
Knit 15 rounds (st st) without shaping. Cast off firmly to ensure that edge rolls to RS.

■ MAKING UP

Press according to instructions on yarn label.
Mark position of sleeves 21[22:23]cm from shoulder seams on back and front.
Sew sleeves to back and front between markers.
Join right front and right back insets.
Join left front and left back insets.
Sew insets to back and front, matching straight end of inset with lower edge of back and front with shaped end approx 8[9:10]cm from lower sleeve edge.

■ LOWER EDGING

With RS facing, using larger circular needle and A, pick up and K204[212:220] sts evenly around lower edge of back and front.
Purl 6 rounds (rev st st) without shaping.
Cast off firmly to ensure that edge rolls to WS.

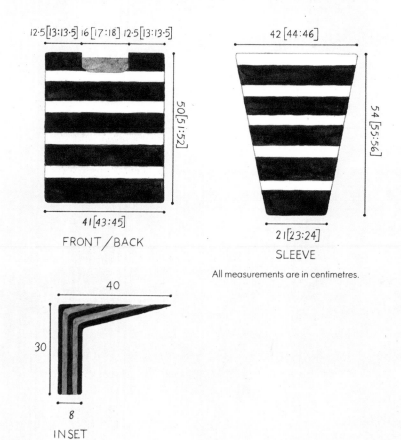

12·5[13:13·5] 16[17:18] 12·5[13:13·5]

50[51:52]

41[43:45]

FRONT/BACK

42[44:46]

54[55:56]

21[23:24]

SLEEVE

All measurements are in centimetres.

40

30

8

INSET

1

2

SIMPLE STRIPE VARIATIONS

The simple but effective transposition of stripes on this design can be used as the basis for any number of different garments. The stripes need not be a consistently standard width; they can be interspersed with a single row of colour as a highlight or follow the colours of the rainbow. By using one colourway horizontally across the back and front and vertical insets as a gusset, you can achieve remarkable visual effects. The samples knitted up here are in soft mellow tones of pink, green, grey, white and black. To help design your own, knit up the striped samples first and play around with them so that you can envisage the end result more clearly.

The patterns for these stripe variations can be incorporated into the master pattern by replacing the stripes with your own width of stripe and number of colours, while maintaining the stocking stitch and shaping throughout. Remember to change the colour on a right side row.

1 2 rows of black between every 2 rows of the other 4 colours – pink, green, white and grey in this sample.
2 10 rows of each colour – grey, pink, green and white – separated by 2 rows of black.
3 Maintaining the 2 rows of black between every colour change, work 4 stripes of each colour, each stripe 2 rows wide.
4 10 rows grey and 2 rows black.

REGATTA

By accenting stripes on part of the design only, this traditional crew neck sweater has been given a 1920s boating air.

▪ SIZE

To fit 86[91:97]cm/34[36:38]in bust
Figures for larger sizes are given in square brackets. Where there is only one set of figures, this applies to all sizes.
See diagram for finished measurements.

▪ MATERIALS

Use a medium weight cotton yarn.
450[450:475]g main colour A (blue)
200g contrast B (maroon)
One pair each of 3mm, 4mm and 5mm knitting needles *or size to obtain correct tension*

▪ TENSION

16 sts and 21 rows to 10cm over st st using largest needles
Check your tension before beginning.

Note

Read chart from right to left for RS knit rows and left to right for WS purl rows.
Unless stated st st is used throughout.
Sleeves are knitted sideways.

▪ FRONT

** Using medium size needles and A, cast on 69[73:77] sts and work 4[6:8] rows in K1, P1 rib.
Change to largest needles and purl one row.
Beg with row 1 of chart and a knit row, work from chart shaping sides by inc one st at each end of 24th, 47th and 70th rows. 75[79:83] sts.
Cont from chart without shaping until end of row 79[77:75].

Armhole shaping

Cast off 3 sts at beg of next 2 rows.
69[73:77] sts.
Dec one st at each end of next and foll 3 alternate rows. 61[65:69] sts. **
Cont from chart without shaping until end of row 126.

Neck shaping

Next row P23[25:27] sts, cast off centre 15 sts, P to end.
Work one row.
Cast off 3 sts at beg of next and foll alternate row. 17[19:21] sts.
Work one row.
Dec one st at neck edge on next and foll alternate row. 15[17:19] sts.
Work 2 rows without shaping.
Cast off.
With RS facing, rejoin yarn to rem sts and work to match first side, reversing shaping.

▪ BACK

Work as for front from ** to **.
Cont without shaping omitting 'V'-shaped striped patt at neck until end of row 134.

Neck shaping

Next row K15[17:19], turn, P to end.
Cast off.
With RS facing, rejoin yarn to rem sts, cast off centre 31 sts, K to end.
Purl one row.
Cast off.

▪ LEFT SLEEVE

Using largest needles and A, cast on 6 sts and beg with a K row, work 2 rows in st st without shaping.
Cast on 5 sts at beg of next and foll alternate row. 16 sts.
*** Cast on 2 sts at beg of next row.
Cast on 5 sts at beg of next row. ***
Rep last 2 rows twice. 37 sts.
Cast on 3 sts at beg of next row.
Cast on 5 sts at beg of next row.
Rep last 2 rows once. 53 sts.
Rep from *** to *** twice. 67 sts.
Inc one st at beg of next row.
Cast on 5 sts at beg of next row.
Rep last 2 rows once. 79 sts.
Inc one st at beg of next and 2 foll alternate rows. 82 sts.
Cont from chart without shaping to end of row 60[61:63].
Dec one st at beg of next and 2 foll alternate rows. 79 sts.
Cast off 5 sts at beg of next row.
Dec one st at beg of next row.
Rep last 2 rows once. 67 sts.
**** Cast off 5 sts at beg of next row.
Cast off 2 sts at beg of next row. ****
Rep last 2 rows once. 53 sts.
Cast off 5 sts at beg of next row.
Cast off 3 sts at beg of next row.
Rep last 2 rows once. 37 sts.
Rep from **** to **** 3 times. 16 sts.
Cast off 5 sts at beg of next and foll alternate row. 6 sts.
Work 2 rows without shaping.
Cast off.

▪ RIGHT SLEEVE

Work as for left sleeve, omitting stripes and working 2nd half of sleeve in B.

▪ FRONT NECKBAND

With RS facing and using smallest needles and A, pick up and K59 sts evenly around front neck.
Work 4 rows in P1, K1 rib.
Cast off evenly in rib.

▪ BACK NECKBAND

With RS facing and using smallest needles and A, pick up and K47 sts evenly around back neck.
Work 4 rows in P1, K1 rib.
Cast off evenly in rib.

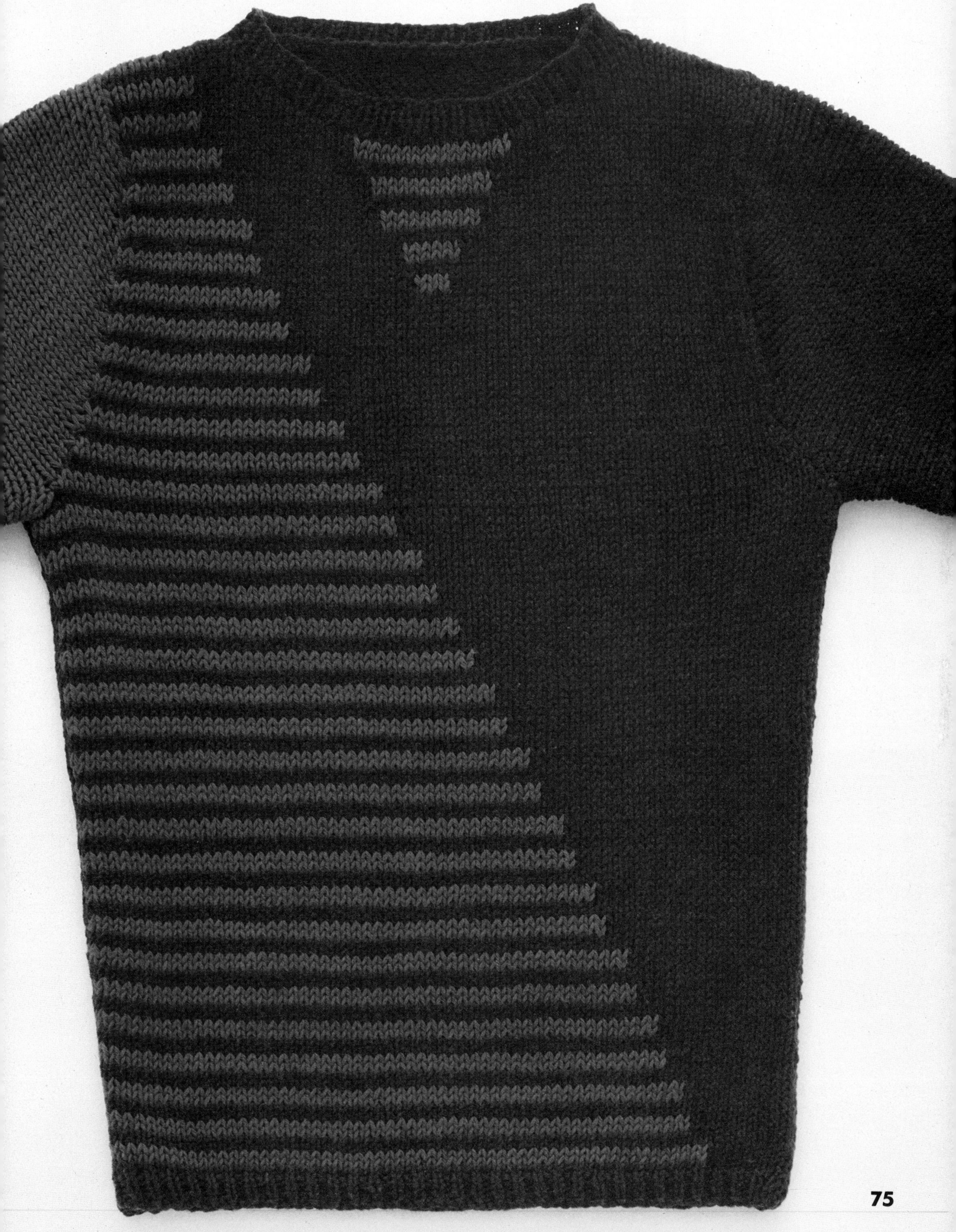

LEFT SLEEVE

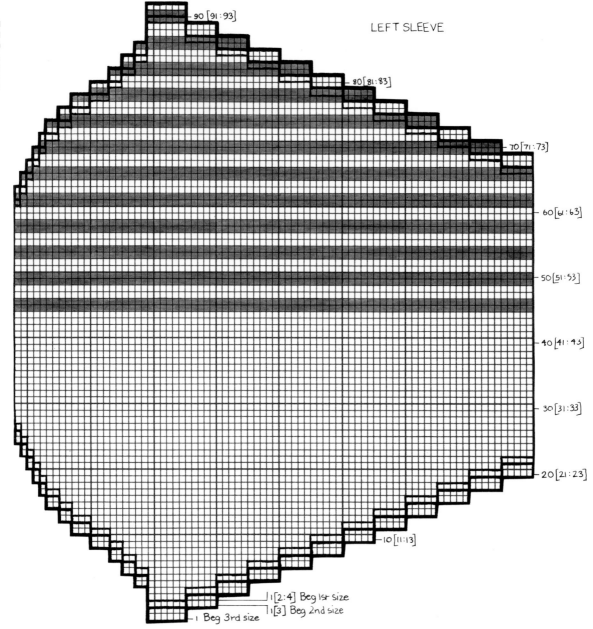

90 [91:93]

80 [81:83]

70 [71:73]

60 [61:63]

50 [51:53]

40 [41:43]

30 [31:33]

20 [21:23]

10 [11:13]

1 [2:4] Beg 1st size
1 [3] Beg 2nd size
1 Beg 3rd size

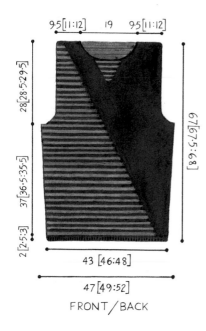

9·5 [11:12]   19   9·5 [11:12]

28 [28·5:29·5]

67 [67·5:68]

37 [36·5:35·5]

2 [2·5:3]

43 [46:48]

47 [49:52]

FRONT / BACK

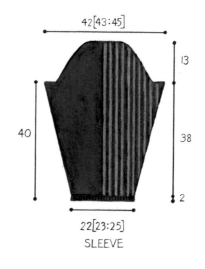

42 [43:45]

13

40

38

2

22 [23:25]

SLEEVE

■ CUFFS
With RS facing and using smallest
needles and A, pick up and K41[43:45]
sts evenly along each cuff.
Work 5 rows in P1, K1 rib.
Cast off.

■ MAKING UP
Press according to instructions on yarn
label.
Join shoulders and neckbands.
Join side and sleeve seams.
Sew in sleeves matching stripes at
head of left sleeve to stripes on back.

All measurements are in centimetres.

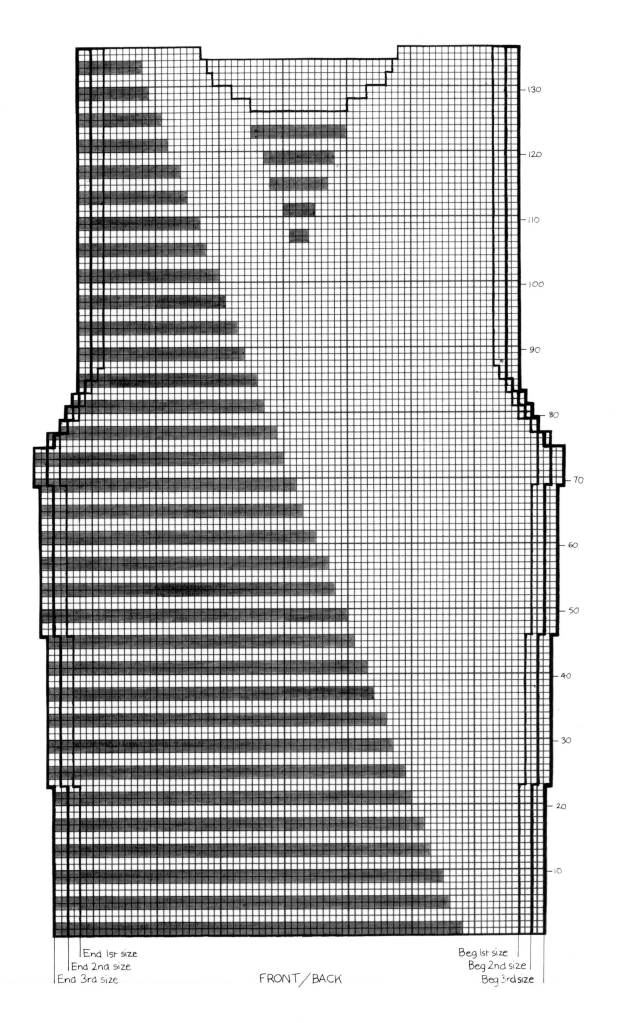

LACE UP

A very simple shape, which can be knitted to any length, and an interesting lace stitch provide the basis for a number of design variations. Experiment by threading other materials through the lace.

■ SIZE

One size to fit up to 97cm/38in bust
See diagram for finished measurements.

■ MATERIALS

Use a lightweight cotton yarn.
280g short top
500g dress version
One pair of 5mm knitting needles *or size to obtain correct tension*

■ TENSION

17 sts and 27 rows to 10cm over patt using 5mm needles
Check your tension before beginning.

BACK AND FRONT (Both alike)

Cast on 86 sts and work in patt as foll:
1st row K3, *yrn, K3, sl 1, K2tog, psso, K3, yrn, K1, rep from * to last 3 sts, K3.
2nd, 4th and 6th rows P.
3rd row K3, *K1, yrn, K2, sl 1, K2tog, psso, K2, yrn, K2, rep from * to last 3 sts, K3.
5th row K3, *K2, yrn, K1, sl 1, K2tog, psso, K1, yrn, K3, rep from * to last 3 sts, K3.
7th row K3, *K3, yrn, sl 1, K2tog, psso, yrn, K4, rep from * to last 3 sts, K3.
8th row P3, K to last 3 sts, P3.
Rep last 8 rows 15 times more.
Next row K.
Next row P.
Cast off.

MAKING UP

Thread colours through the loop formed by psso in the lace pattern and secure at top and bottom of garment on WS.
Join shoulder seams for 10cm, leaving 31cm open for neck.
Join side seams, leaving 25cm open for armhole.
Press garment according to instructions on yarn label.

DRESS VERSION

To extend lace patt for dress, cont in patt until you reach the desired length.
Next row (RS) K.
Next row P.
Cast off.

MAKING UP

As for short version.

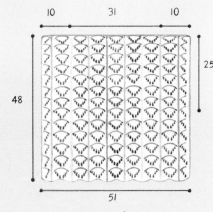

FRONT / BACK

All measurements are in centimetres.

CHANGING THREADS

By using different fabrics and threading them through the lace pattern in different ways, you can create a variety of effects with this simple top.

1 Find the ridge of purl stitches which form the tops of the lace V and run the yarn through the bottom loop of the stitch and over to form an overstitch across the garment. To make tassels, take three lengths of yarn, each 10cm long, and thread them through the two holes at the bottom of the lace V. Tie them lightly in a double knot and cut the ends 2cm from the knot.

2 Cut lengths of fabric into 2cm strips. Press in half lengthwise and thread across the garment through all the holes of the lace V.

3 Use two strands of yarn and take them across the garment through all the holes of the lace V.

4 In this neutral colourway, the yarns have been threaded double in the same way as the threads on the main design.

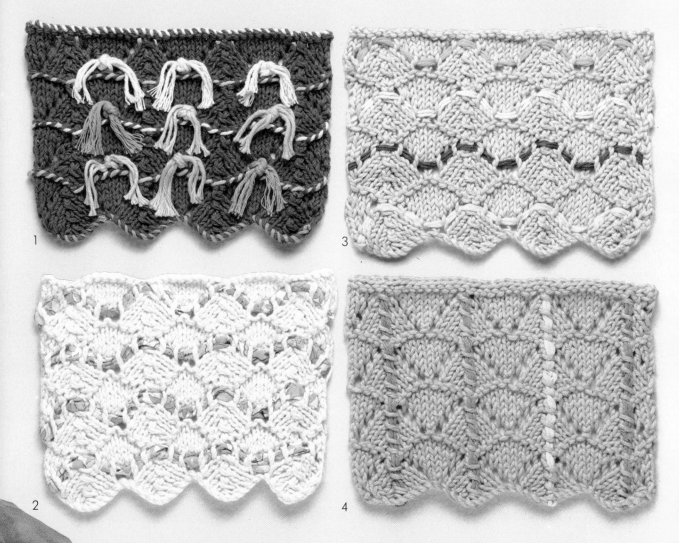

1

2

3

4

TIGER TAILS

Tails of toning colours wind across this batwing sweater, producing an exciting contrast with the background. The contrasting colours in the tails have been used again as an edge to the ribbed bands.

■ SIZE

One size to fit up to 91cm/36in bust
See diagram for finished measurements.

■ MATERIALS

Use a lightweight cotton slub yarn for the main colour and lightweight and medium weight cotton yarns for the contrast in either bouclé, slub, plain or mercerised.

500g main colour A (brown)
50g each in 10 toning colours B,C,D,E,F,G,H,J,L,N (blue)
One 2.50mm crochet hook
One pair each of 3¾mm and 4½mm knitting needles (or circular knitting needle if preferred) *or size to obtain correct tension*

■ TENSION

18 sts and 24 rows to 10cm over st st using larger needles
Check your tension before beginning.

Note

The main colour (A) is used double throughout; the other yarns are used in combination or singly.
Use separate balls of yarn for each area, do not carry yarn across back of work. Take care to twist yarns at the back when changing colours to avoid holes forming (see page 114). Read chart from right to left for RS knit rows and left to right for WS purl rows.
Unless stated st st is used throughout.
This garment is worked in one piece.

■ BODY

Back

Using smaller needles and F, cast on 81 sts, change to A and work in rib as foll:
1st rib row (RS) K1, *P1, K1, rep from * to end.
2nd rib row P1, *K1, P1, rep from * to end.
Rep last 2 rows 6 times.
15th rib row As first rib row.
Inc row Rib 2, (M1, rib 2) 39 times, rib 1. 120 sts.

Change to larger needles, and beg with a K row, work in st st from row 1 of chart for 34 rows.

Sleeve shaping

Cont in patt, cast on 5 sts at beg of next 20 rows. 220 sts.
Cont without shaping to end of row 102.

Neck shaping

Next row Patt 97 sts, turn and leave rem sts on a spare needle.
**Cast off 6 at beg of next row and 4 sts on foll alternate row. Work one row. Inc one st at beg of next and foll alternate row.
Work one row.
Inc 2 sts at beg of next and foll alternate row.
Work one row.
Inc 3 sts at beg of next row.
Work one row.
Inc 4 sts at beg of next row.**

Work one row. 100 sts.
Leave these sts on a spare needle.
With RS facing, rejoin yarn A to rem sts, cast off 26 sts and patt to end.
P one row.
Work from ** to ** as for first side, ending with a K row.
Next row P to end, cast on 20 sts, P across sts of first side from spare needle. 220 sts.
Cont without shaping down front until end of row 160.

Sleeve shaping
Cast off 5 sts at beg of next 20 rows.
120 sts.
Cont without shaping to end of chart.
Change to smaller needles and A only.
Next row K1, P1, (K2tog, P1) to last st,
K1. 81 sts.
Beg with 2nd row, work in rib as for
back for 15 rows.
Change to F and work one row in rib.
Cast off in F.

■ **CUFFS** (Make 2)
Using smaller needles and A, pick up
53 sts evenly along end of sleeve and
work in P1, K1 rib for 15 rows.
Change to F and work one row in rib.
Cast off in F.

■ **NECK EDGING**
Using A singly, work 2 rows of double
crochet evenly around neck edge.

■ **MAKING UP**
Press lightly on WS.
Join side and underarm seams.

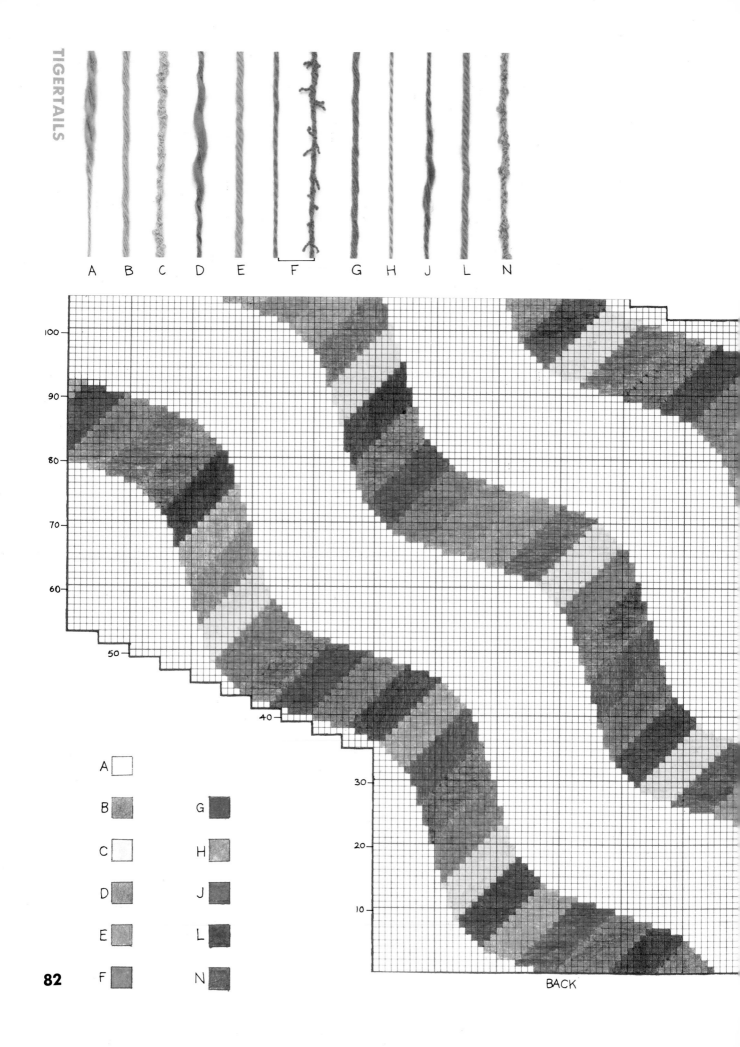

A B C D E F G H J L N

A
B   G
C   H
D   J
E   L
82   F   N

100
90
80
70
60
50
40
30
20
10

BACK

Chart continues on pages 84 and 85

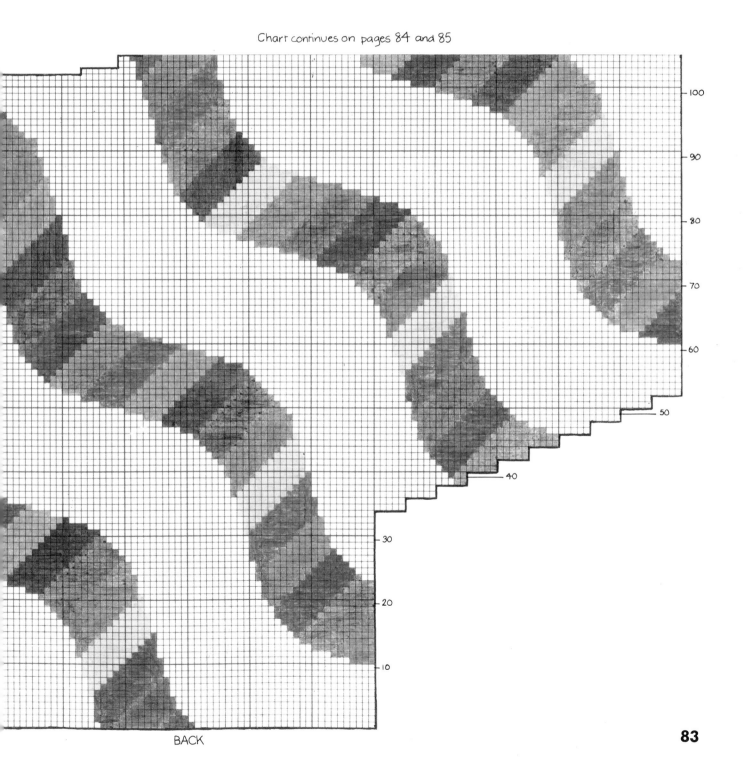

BACK

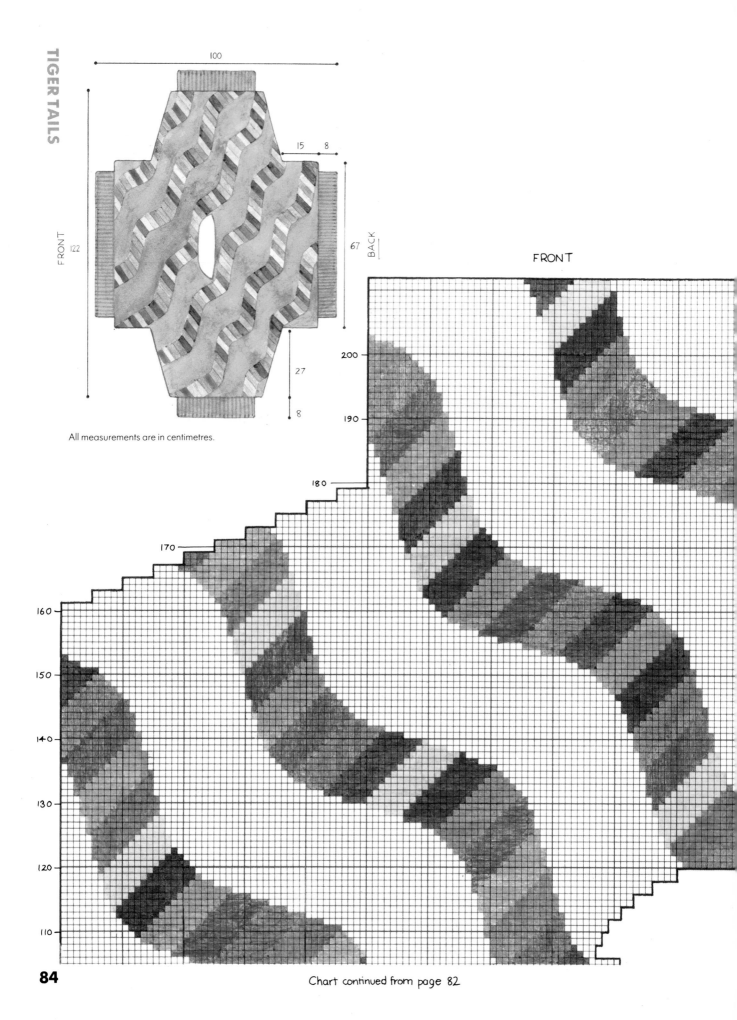

100

15   8

FRONT   122

BACK   67

27

8

200

190

180

170

160

150

140

130

120

110

FRONT

All measurements are in centimetres.

Chart continued from page 82

FRONT

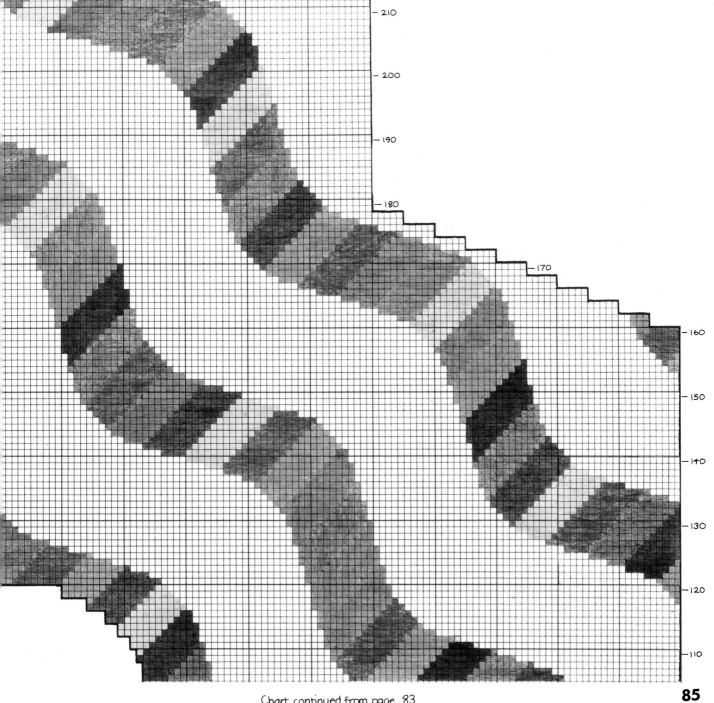

— 210

— 200

— 190

— 180

— 170

— 160

— 150

— 140

— 130

— 120

— 110

Chart continued from page 83

85

SWEET CHESTNUT

A variety of faggot and eyelet stitches has been used in this short-sleeved top. A pastel colourway would emphasize the stitch pattern.

■ SIZE
One size to fit up to 102cm/40in bust
See diagram for finished measurements.

■ MATERIALS
250g lightweight cotton yarn
One pair each of 3¼mm and 4mm knitting needles *or size to obtain correct tension*
Three 15-20mm buttons

■ TENSION
24 sts and 30 rows to 10cm over patt using larger needles
Check your tension before beginning.

■ BACK
Using smaller needles, cast on 125 sts and work in rib as foll:
1st rib row (RS) K1, *P1, K1, rep from * to end.
2nd rib row P1, *K1, P1, rep from * to end.

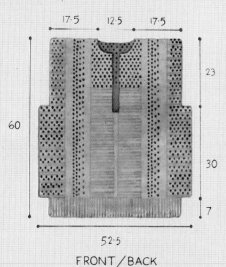

17·5   12·5   17·5

23

60

30

7

52·5

FRONT/BACK

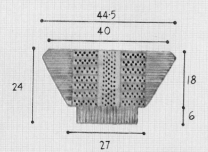

44·5

40

24

18

6

27

SLEEVE

3
10

10·5
POCKET

All measurements are in centimetres.

Rep last 2 rows until rib measures 7cm, ending with a 2nd row, inc one st in last row. 126 sts.
Change to larger needles and work in patt as foll:
1st row K4, P1, (K1, yfwd, K2tog) 5 times, K1, P1, K2, P1, K12, yfwd, K2tog, K2, P1, K2, (P18, K2) twice, P1, K12, yfwd, K2tog, (K2, P1) twice, (K1, yfwd, K2tog) 5 times, K1, P1, K4.
2nd row P2, (P2, K1, P16, K1) twice, P42, (K1, P16, K1, P2) twice, P2.
3rd row K4, P1, K2, (K1, yfwd, K2tog) 4 times, (K2, P1) twice, K10, yfwd, K2tog, K4, P1, K2, (P18, K2) twice, P1, K10, yfwd, K2tog, K4, P1, K2, P1, K2, (K1, yfwd, K2tog) 4 times, K2, P1, K4.
4th row As 2nd row.
5th row K4, P1, K16, P1, K2, P1, K8, (yfwd, K2tog, K2) twice, P1, K2, (P18, K2) twice, P1, K8, (yfwd, K2tog, K2) twice, P1, K2, P1, K16, P1, K4.
6th row P4, K18, P2, K1, P16, K1, P2, (K18, P2) twice, K1, P16, K1, P2, K18, P4.
7th row K4, P1, K16, P1, K2, P1, K6, (yfwd, K2tog, K2) twice, K2, P1, K2, (P18, K2) twice, P1, K6, (yfwd, K2tog, K2) twice, (K2, P1) twice, K16, P1, K4.
8th row As 2nd row.
These 8 rows form patt.
Cont without shaping until back measures 37cm, ending with a WS row.

Shape armholes
Cast off 6 sts at beg of next 2 rows. 114 sts.
Cont without shaping *working 4 sts in st st at each end of row* until armhole measures 13cm, ending with a WS row.
Using st markers, mark positions of 16 central sts of each of 2 central panels. Keeping to patt as set on all sts but the 2 sets of 16 sts, work mesh st over these 2 sets of 16 sts on next 4 rows as foll:
1st row (RS) (K1, yfwd, K2tog) 5 times, K1.
2nd row P.
3rd row K2, (K1, yfwd, K2tog) 4 times, K2.
4th row P.
These 4 rows form mesh patt.
Cont in patt as set until armhole measures 21cm.

Neck shaping
Next row Patt 45 sts, turn and leave rem sts on a spare needle.
Dec one st at neck edge on next and 2 foll alternate rows. 42 sts.
Cast off.
With RS facing, rejoin yarn to rem sts. Cast off centre 24 sts, work to match first side, reversing shaping.

■ FRONT
Work as for back until front measures 33cm.

Divide front
Next row Patt 63 sts, turn and leave rem sts on a spare needle.
Cont on these 63 sts without shaping *keeping 3 sts at neck edge in st st*, until front measures same as back to armhole, ending with a WS row.

Shape armhole
Cast off 6 sts at beg of next row. 57 sts.
Cont without shaping until armhole measures 5cm, ending with a WS row.
Now working central panel of 16 sts in mesh st, cont without shaping until front measures 17 rows less than back to shoulder.

Neck shaping
Cast off 11 sts at beg of next row.
Work 3 rows.
Dec one st (3 sts in from edge) on next and foll 4th row 3 times. 42 sts.
Cast off.
With RS facing, rejoin yarn to rem sts and work to match first side, reversing shapings.

■ SLEEVES (Make 2)
Using smaller needles, cast on 65 sts and work in rib as for back for 6cm, inc one st in last row. 66 sts.
Change to larger needles and work in 8 row patt as foll *and at the same time* shape sides by inc one st at each end (4 sts in from edge) of 3rd and every foll alternate row until there are 107 sts, working inc sts in mesh patt as for central panels on back and front.
1st row K4, P1, *(K1, yfwd, K2tog) 5 times, K1, P1, K2, P1, * rep from * to * once, (K1, yfwd, K2tog) 5 times, K1, P1, K4.
2nd row P2, (P2, K1, P16, K1) 3 times, P4.
3rd row K4, P1, K2, *(K1, yfwd, K2tog) 4 times, K2, P1, K2, P1, K2,* rep from * to * once, (K1, yfwd, K2tog) 4 times, K2, P1, K4.
4th row As 2nd row.
5th row K4, P1, K16, P1, K2, P1, (K1, yfwd, K2tog) 5 times, K1, P1, K2, P1, K16, P1, K4.
6th row P4, K18, P2, K1, P16, K1, P2, K18, P4.
7th row K4, P1, K16, P1, K2, P1, K2, (K1, yfwd, K2tog) 4 times, K2, P1, K2, P1, K16, P1, K4.
8th row As 2nd row.
Work without shaping until sleeve measures 22cm, ending with a RS row.
Dec one st at each end of next 5 rows.
Cast off.

■ POCKET
Using larger needles, cast on 25 sts and work in mesh st for 10cm.

Change to smaller needles and work in K1, P1 rib for 3cm.
Cast off.

▓ PLACKETS (Make 2)

With RS facing, using smaller needles, pick up and K30 sts down button side of front opening.
Work 6 rows in K1, P1 rib.
Cast off.
Work buttonhole side as for button side with the addition of 3 buttonholes on 3rd row as foll:
Rib 4, (K2tog, yfwd, rib 8) twice, K2tog, yfwd, rib 4.

▓ COLLAR

Join shoulder seams.
With RS facing, using smaller needles, beg at 3rd row of placket, pick up and K113 sts evenly around neck ending at 3rd row of placket.
Work in K1, P1 rib for 9cm, dec one st (4 sts in from edge) on every 4th row.
Cast off.

▓ MAKING UP

Do not press.
Place centre of cast off edge of sleeve to shoulder seam and join back to front at underarm.
Join side and sleeve seams.
Sew on pocket.
Sew on buttons.

CRAZY PAVING

Random shapes of colour in vibrant red are separated from each other by wide strips of black to resemble paving stones. The high wrap-over shawl collar gives the garment a quiet sophistication.

SIZE

To fit 81-86[91-97]cm/32-34[36-38]in bust
Figures for larger sizes are given in square brackets. Where there is only one set of figures, this applies to all sizes.
See diagram for finished measurements.

MATERIALS

Use a lightweight cotton yarn double throughout or a medium weight yarn singly.
500[550]g main colour A (red)
300[325]g contrast B (black)
One pair each of 3mm and 3¾mm knitting needles *or size to obtain correct tension*

TENSION

24 sts and 32 rows to 10cm over patt using larger needles
Check your tension before beginning.

Note

Read chart from right to left for RS rows and left to right for WS rows.
Use separate ball of yarn for each area. Do not carry yarn not in use across back of work (see page 114).

STITCHES

Moss st (Main colour A)
Worked over even number of sts.
1st row *K1, P1, rep from * to end.
2nd row *P1, K1, rep from * to end.
These 2 rows form patt.

Worked over odd number of sts.
1st row *K1, *P1, K1, rep from * to end.
This row forms patt.

Stocking st (Colour B)
1st row (RS) K.
2nd row P.
These 2 rows form patt.

BACK

Using smaller needles, cast on 18[23]A, 8B, 24A, 11B, 45A, 5B, 19[24]A. 130[140] sts.
Keeping to colours as set, work in rib as foll:
1st rib row (RS) K1, *P1, K1, rep from * to end.
2nd rib row P1, *K1, P1, rep from * to end.
Rep last 2 rib rows 12 times.
Change to larger needles and work in patt from chart.
Place a marker at each end of row 90[106].
Cont without shaping to end of row 180[196].
Cast off.

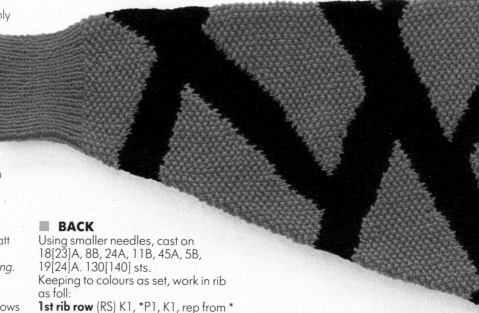

FRONT

Work as for back to end of row 100[118].

Neck shaping

Next row Patt 77[85] sts, turn and leave rem sts on a spare needle.
Keeping side edge straight, shape neck by inc at centre front edge as indicated on chart until there are 87[92] sts.
Cont without shaping to end of row 180[196].

Shoulder shaping

Cast off 43[48] sts at beg of next row and cont without shaping on rem 44 sts to end of chart.
With RS facing, rejoin yarns to rem 53[55] sts, cast on 24[30] sts and work to match first side, reversing shapings.

SLEEVES (Make 2)

Using smaller needles, cast on 14A, 11B, 33A. 58 sts.
Work in rib as for back for 26 rows.
Change to larger needles and work in patt from chart, shaping sides by inc one st at each end of 3rd and every foll 3rd row until there are 134 sts. Cont without shaping to end of chart.
Cast off.

MAKING UP

Press according to instructions on yarn label.
Join shoulder seams.
Sew cast off edge of sleeves to front and back between markers.
Join side and sleeve seams.
Join collar at back neck and sew to back neck of body.
Fold collar to wrong side and stitch down.

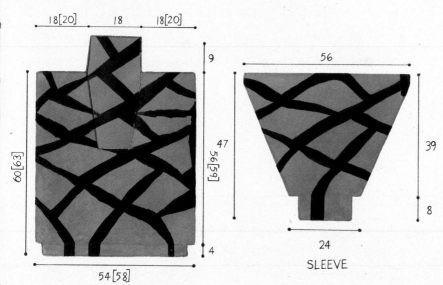

FRONT/BACK

SLEEVE

All measurements are in centimetres.

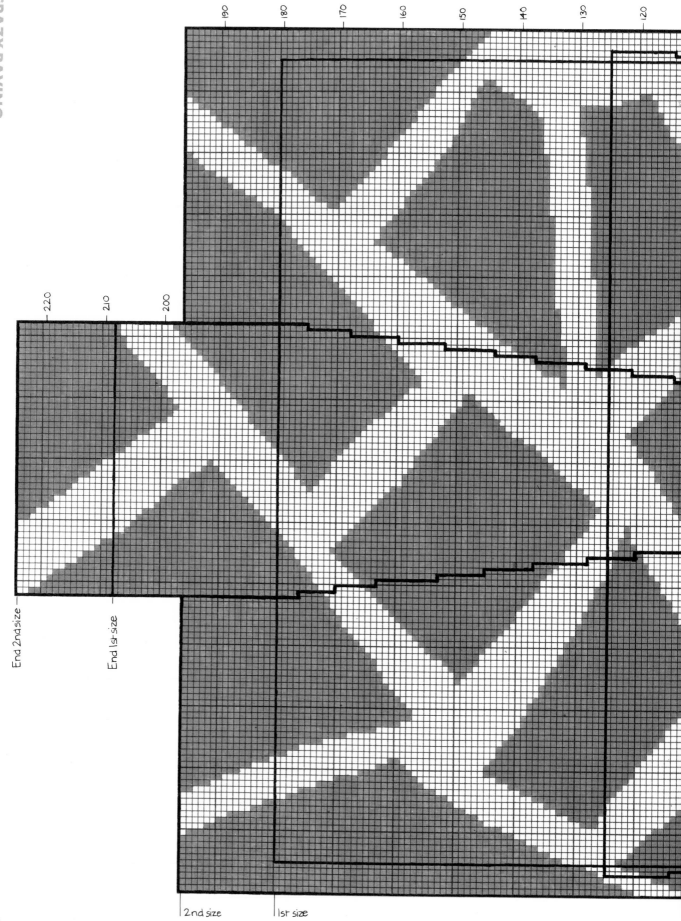

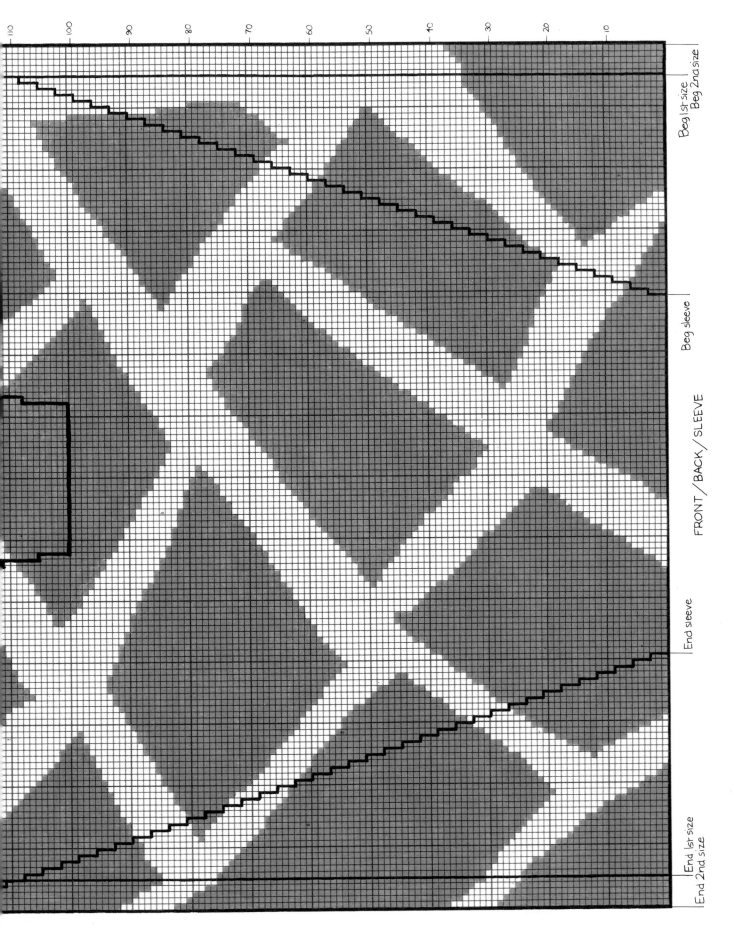

BLOCKBUSTER

Primary blocks of colour provide the background for this striped short-sleeved sweater. Because the yarn in the stripe is woven across the back of the work, it knits up into a closely worked fabric. Long sleeves turn it into a warm winter garment.

■ **SIZE**
To fit 81[86:91:97-102]cm/ 32[34:36:38-40]in bust
Figures for larger sizes are given in square brackets. Where there is only one set of figures, this applies to all sizes.

See diagram for finished measurements.

■ **MATERIALS**
Use a lightweight cotton slub yarn. 350[375:375:400]g main colour A (blue)
75[75:100:100]g 1st contrast B (red)
75[75:100:100]g 2nd contrast C (yellow)

150[150:175:175]g 3rd contrast D (white)
Long sleeve version:
450[475:475:500]g main colour A
One pair each of 3mm and 3¾mm knitting needles *or size to obtain correct tension*

■ TENSION

23 sts and 28 rows to 10cm over stripe patt using larger needles
Check your tension before beginning.

Note

Carry D across back of work, weaving with other colour every 2 or 3 sts (see page 114).

■ BACK

Using smaller needles and A, cast on 113[119:125:131] sts and work in rib as foll:
1st rib row (RS) K1, *P1, K1, rep from * to end.
2nd rib row P1, *K1, P1, rep from * to end.
Rep last 2 rows 3 times, inc one st in last row. 114[120:126:132] sts.
Change to larger needles and work in patt as foll:
1st row K5[2:5:2]B, (K1D, K5B) 8[9:9:10] times, K1D, K3B, K3A, K1D, (K5A, K1D) 8[9:9:10] times, K5[2:5:2]A.
2nd row P5[2:5:2]A, (P1D, P5A) 8[9:9:10] times, P1D, P3A, P3B, P1D, (P5B, P1D) 8[9:9:10] times, P5[2:5:2]B.
These 2 rows form patt.
Cont without shaping until end of row 50[51:52:53].
Change colour B for C and cont without shaping until end of row 76, place a marker at each end of this row for armhole.
Cont without shaping until end of row 100[102:104:106].
Change colour C for A and cont without shaping until work measures 22[23:24:25]cm from armhole marker, ending with a WS row.

Shoulder shaping

Cast off 6[6:6:0] sts at beg of next 12[8:4:0] rows. 42[72:102:132] sts.
Cast off 0[7:7:7] sts at beg of next 0[4:8:12] rows.
Cast off rem 42[44:46:48] sts.

■ FRONT

Work as for back until front measures 12[14:16:18] rows less than back to shoulder shaping.

Neck shaping

Next row Patt 46[48:51:53] sts, turn and leave rem sts on a spare needle.
Cast off 3 sts at beg of next row.
Knit one row.
Cast off 2 sts at beg of next and foll alternate rows.
Knit one row.
Dec one st at beg of next and foll 2[2:3:3] alternate rows.
Work 0[2:0:2] rows without shaping. 36[38:40:42] sts.

Shoulder shaping

Cast off 6[6:6:0] sts at beg of next and foll 5[3:1:0] alternate rows.
Work one row.
Cast off 0[7:7:7] sts at beg of next and foll 0[1:3:5] alternate rows.
With RS facing rejoin yarn to rem sts, cast off centre 22[24:24:26] sts, patt to end.
Work to match first side reversing shaping.

■ SLEEVES (Make 2)

**Using smaller needles and A, cast on 77[81:83:85] sts and work in rib as for back for 8 rows.
Change to larger needles and patt as foll:
1st row K2[1:2:3]A, (K1D, K5A) 12[13:13:13] times, K1D, K2[1:2:3]A. This row places stripes**.
Cont in patt *and at the same time* shape sides by inc one st at each end of 5th[5th:5th:4th] and every foll 5th[5th:4th:4th] row 13[13:14:16] times in all, taking inc sts into patt. 103[107:111:117] sts.
Work without shaping until sleeve measures 28[29:30:31]cm from beg, ending with a WS row.
Cast off.

■ COLLAR

Using smaller needles and with RS facing and A, beg at centre front and pick up and K99[103:107:111] sts evenly around neck using a 3rd needle for ease of working.
Work in rib as for back for 21 rows.
Cast off.

■ MAKING UP

Join centre front of collar for 1cm from neck edge. Press lightly under a cloth.
Join shoulder seams.
Sew sleeves between markers.
Join sleeve and side seams.

LONG SLEEVE VERSION

■ FRONT AND BACK

Work as for short sleeve version.

■ SLEEVES (Make 2)

Work as for short sleeve version from ** to **.
Cont in patt *and at the same time* shape sides by inc one st at each end of every 9th[9th:8th:7th and 8th alternately]row 13[13:14:16] times in all, taking inc sts into patt. 103[107:111:117] sts.
Work without shaping until sleeve measures 45cm, ending with a WS row.
Cast off.

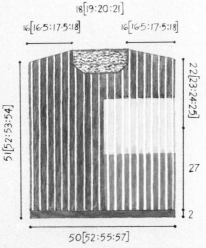

18[19:20:21]

16[16.5:17.5:18]   16[16.5:17.5:18]

51[52:53:54]

22[23:24:25]

27

2

50[52:55:57]

FRONT/BACK

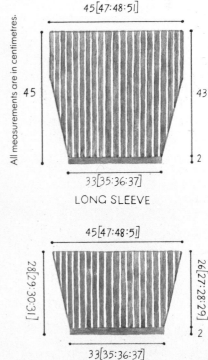

All measurements are in centimetres.

45[47:48:51]

45

43

2

33[35:36:37]

LONG SLEEVE

45[47:48:51]

28[29:30:31]

26[27:28:29]

2

33[35:36:37]

SHORT SLEEVE

BASKETWEAVE

The pattern on this sweater is achieved by the simple technique of slipping stitches. This is one of the easiest ways to create a textured stripe.

◼ SIZE

To fit 86[91:97]cm/34[36:38]in bust
Figures for larger sizes are given in square brackets. Where there is only one set of figures, this applies to all sizes.
See diagram for finished measurements.

◼ MATERIALS

Use a lightweight cotton yarn and cotton bouclé.
400[400:450]g bouclé A (natural)
250g 1st contrast B (slate)
50g 2nd contrast C (blue)
50g 3rd contrast D (light blue)
One each of 3mm and 3¾mm circular knitting needle *or size to obtain correct tension*

◼ TENSION

22 sts and 40 rows to 10cm over patt using larger needle
Check your tension before beginning.

Note

Body of garment is worked in one piece to armhole.

◼ BODY

Using smaller needle and B, cast on 220[236:252] sts and work in rounds of K2, P2 for 7cm.
Change to larger needle and D, knit one round, inc 4 sts evenly.
224[240:256] sts.
Using D, purl one round.
Beg patt as foll:
1st round Using A, K.
2nd round Using A, P.
3rd round Using C, K2, *with yarn at back of work sl 2 p-wise, K6, rep from * to last 6 sts, sl 2 p-wise, K4.
4th to 6th rounds As 3rd round.
7th and 8th rounds As first and 2nd rounds.
9th round As first round.
10th to 12th rounds As 2nd round.
Rep these 12 rounds without shaping until work measures 40cm from beg, using colours C, D and B for 3rd to 6th rounds in rotation.

Back

Divide for armholes as foll:
Keeping patt correct as set, work back and forth across first 112[120:128] sts for back, changing WS rows to K or P as appropriate and leaving rem sts on a spare needle.
Cont on these sts until armhole measures 25cm, ending with a WS row in A.

Front

Rejoin yarn to rem sts on spare needle and work as for back until armhole measures 16cm.

Neck shaping

Next row Patt 41[45:49] sts, turn and leave rem sts on a spare needle.
Dec one st at neck edge on every row until 21[25:29] sts rem.
Work without shaping until front measures same as back.

Leave these 21[25:29] sts on a spare needle.
With RS facing, rejoin yarn to rem sts, cast off centre 30 sts and patt to end.
Work to match first side, reversing shaping.
Join shoulders as foll:
Place 21[25:29] sts of front shoulder parallel with 21[25:29] sts of

corresponding back shoulder with WS together and using a 3rd needle and A, K through back and front and cast off, thus forming a ridge on RS.

◼ NECKBAND

With RS facing and using smaller circular needle and B, K70 sts from back neck, pick up and K20 sts down left side of neck, K30 sts across front and K20 sts up right side of neck. 140 sts.
Work in K2, P2 rib for 12 rounds.
Cast off in rib.

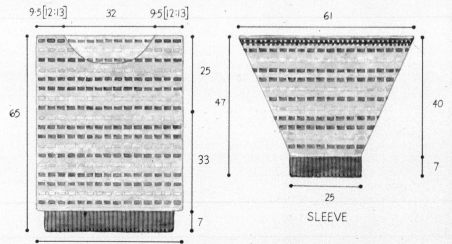

9·5[12:13] 32 9·5[12:13]

25

65

47

33

7

51[54:58]

FRONT / BACK

61

40

7

25

SLEEVE

All measurements are in centimetres.

94

SLEEVES (Make 2)

With RS facing and using larger circular needle and D, beg at start of armhole and pick up and K134 sts evenly around armhole and work back and forth as foll:

1st row Using D, K.

2nd and 3rd rows Using C, K.

4th row Using D, K2, * with yarn at back of work sl 2 p-wise, K2, rep from * to end.

5th row Using D, P2, * with yarn at front of work sl 2 p-wise, P2, rep from * to end.

6th and 7th rows As 4th and 5th rows.

8th and 9th rows Using B, K.

Using B in place of D, rep rows 2 to 7. Now change to patt as for body using 3rd colour for stripe *and keeping patt correct*, dec one st at each end of next and every foll 4th row until sleeve measures approx 40cm, ending with an 8th patt row.

Change to smaller needle and D, knit one row dec evenly to 54 sts.

Using D, knit one row.

Change to B, knit one row.

Work in rib as foll:

1st row (WS) P2, *K2, P2, rep from * to end.

2nd row K2, *P2, K2, rep from * to end.

Rep these 2 rows until work measures 7cm, ending with a first row. Cast off.

MAKING UP

Press lightly on WS.

Join sleeve seams, matching patt.

PRIMARY CABLES

Cables in primary colours provide these vertical stripes. A tailless version is given too.

■ SIZE

One size to fit up to 97cm/38in bust
See diagram for finished measurements.

■ MATERIALS

Use a lightweight yarn.
650g main colour A (white)
100g 1st contrast B (yellow)
50g 2nd contrast C (red)
50g 3rd contrast D (blue)
One pair each of 2¾mm and 3¼mm knitting needles *or size to obtain correct tension*
One cable needle

■ TENSION

24 sts and 32 rows to 10cm over patt using larger needles
Check your tension before beginning.

Note
Use separate ball of contrast colour for each cable panel, twisting colours at back of work to avoid holes forming (see page 114).

■ FRONT

Using larger needles and A, cast on 148 sts and work in rev st st and cable patt as foll:
1st row P19A, K6B, P20A, K6C, P20A, K6B, P20A, K6D, P20A, K6C, P19A.
2nd row and every alternate row
K19A, (P6 in contrast colour, K20A) 4 times, P6 in contrast colour, K19A.
3rd and 4th rows As first and 2nd rows.
5th row P19A, slip next 3 sts onto cable needle and leave at back of work,

K3B, K3B from cable needle – called C6 –, P20A, C6C, P20A, C6B, P20A, C6D, P20A, C6C, P19A.
6th row As 2nd row.
These 6 rows form patt.
Cont in patt without shaping until work measures 32cm.
Place a marker at each end of last row.
Cont in patt without shaping until work measures 50cm, ending with a WS row.

Neck shaping
Next row Patt 60 sts, turn and leave rem sts on a spare needle.
Cast off 6 sts at neck end of next row.
Work one row.
Cast off 3 sts at neck end of next row.
Work one row.
Cast off 2 sts at neck end of next row.
Work one row.
Dec one st at neck edge on next and 3 foll alternate rows. 45 sts.

Shoulder shaping
Cast off 7 sts at beg of next and 2 foll alternate rows.
Work one row.
Cast off 6 sts at beg of next and 3 foll alternate rows.
With RS facing, rejoin yarn to rem sts, cast off centre 28 sts and work to match first side, reversing shaping.

■ BACK

Using larger needles and A, cast on 22 sts.
1st row Cast on 3 sts, P8A, K6B, P8A.
This row sets centre cable, placing further cables as front when sufficient sts have been inc, cont in patt and cast on 3 sts at beg of next 21 rows. 88 sts.
Cast on 2 sts at beg of next 30 rows. 148 sts.
Place a marker at each end of last row.
Cont without shaping until back measures (from markers) the same as front to shoulder shaping.

Shoulder shaping
Cast off 7 sts at beg of next 6 rows. 106 sts.
Cast off 6 sts at beg of next 8 rows. 58 sts.
Cast off.

■ SLEEVES (Make 2)

Using smaller needles and A, cast on 83 sts and work in rib as foll:
1st rib row (RS) K1, *P1, K1, rep from * to end.
2nd rib row P1, *K1, P1, rep from * to end.
Rep 2 rib rows 3 times.
Change to larger needles and cable patt as foll:
1st row P1A, K6B, P19A, K6D, P19A, K6B, P19A, K6C, P1A.
This row places cables.
Keeping patt correct and taking inc sts into rev st st only, shape sides by inc one st at each end of 5th and every foll 6th row until there are 129 sts.
Cont without shaping until sleeve measures 50cm, ending with a WS row. Cast off.

■ NECKBAND

Join right shoulder seam.
With RS facing and using smaller needles and A, pick up and K127 sts evenly around neck edge.
Work 8 rows in rib as for sleeve.
Cast off evenly in rib.

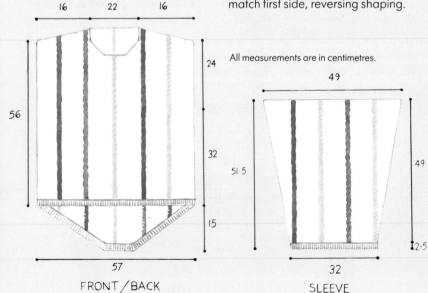

All measurements are in centimetres.

16 22 16

24

56

32

15

57

FRONT/BACK

49

51·5

49

2·5

32

SLEEVE

◼ BACK WELT

With RS facing and using smaller needles and A, pick up and K173 sts around tail between markers.
Work 8 rows in rib as for sleeve.
Cast off evenly in rib.

◼ FRONT WELT

With RS facing and using smaller needles and A, pick up and K129 sts across cast on edge.
Work 8 rows in rib as for sleeve.
Cast off evenly in rib.

◼ MAKING UP

Join left shoulder, using 10mm wide tape along the seam (see page 118).
Press lightly on WS avoiding ribbing.
Sew sleeves to back and front between markers.
Join side and sleeve seams.

TAILLESS VERSION

◼ BACK

Work as for front, omitting neck shaping until back measures same as front to shoulder shaping.
Shape shoulders as for tail version.

COVER STORY

This versatile design can be worn either as a cardigan or as a beach cover-up. The textured cotton yarn is knitted in to give a towelling effect.

■ SIZE

One size to fit up to 102cm/40in bust
See diagram for finished measurements.

■ MATERIALS

Use a medium weight cotton yarn and fine towelling yarn.
500g main colour A (beige)
300g 1st contrast B (yellow)
250g towelling yarn C (beige)
For longer version:
550g main colour A
350g 1st contrast B
300g towelling yarn C
One pair each of 4mm and 5½mm knitting needles *or size to obtain correct tension*

■ TENSION

19 sts and 30 rows to 10cm over patt using larger needles
Check your tension before beginning.

■ BACK

Using smaller needles and A, cast on 109 sts and work in rib as foll:
1st rib row K1A, *P1B, K1A, rep from * to end.
2nd rib row P1A, *K1B, P1A, rep from * to end.
Rep last 2 rows until rib measures 8cm, ending with a 2nd row.
Change to larger needles and work in patt as foll:
1st row K, using A.
2nd row K, using A.
3rd row K, using C.
4th row P, using C.
5th row P, using B.
6th row K, using B.
7th row K, using C.
8th row P, using C.
These 8 rows form patt.
Cont in patt without shaping until back measures 47cm, ending with a WS row.

Armhole shaping

Cast off 8 sts at beg of next 2 rows. 93 sts.
Cont in patt without shaping until armhole measures 19cm, ending with a WS row.

Neck shaping

Next row Patt 34 sts, turn and leave rem sts on a spare needle.
Dec one st at neck edge on next and 4 foll alternate rows. 29 sts.
Cast off using A.
With RS facing, rejoin yarn to rem sts, cast off centre 25 sts and work to

match first side, reversing shaping.

■ LEFT FRONT

Using smaller needles and A, cast on 45 sts and work in rib as for back.
Change to larger needles and work in stripe patt until front measures 43cm, ending with a RS row.

Front edge shaping

Dec one st at beg of next row and at front edge on every 9th row 7 times *and at the same time* cast off 8 sts at armhole edge when front measures same as back to armhole. 29 sts.
Cont without shaping until front measures same as back to shoulder.
Cast off using A only.

■ RIGHT FRONT

Work as for left front, reversing shapings.

■ SLEEVES (Make 2)

Using smaller needles and A, cast on 45 sts and work in rib as for back.
Change to larger needles and work in stripe patt, shaping sides by inc one st at each end of every 3rd row 28 times. 101 sts.
Cont without shaping until sleeve measures 47cm.

Top shaping

Dec one st at each end of every alternate row 4 times. 93 sts.
Cast off using A only.

■ NECK BORDER

(Worked in 2 halves)
Join shoulder seams.
With RS facing and using smaller needles and A, pick up and K109 sts up right front and across half of back neck.
Work in rib as for back for 10cm, beg with a 2nd row.
Cast off in rib using A only.
Work 2nd half of border beg at back neck.

■ BELT

Using larger needles and A, cast on 18 sts and work in rib as for back for 170cm.
Cast off in rib using A only.

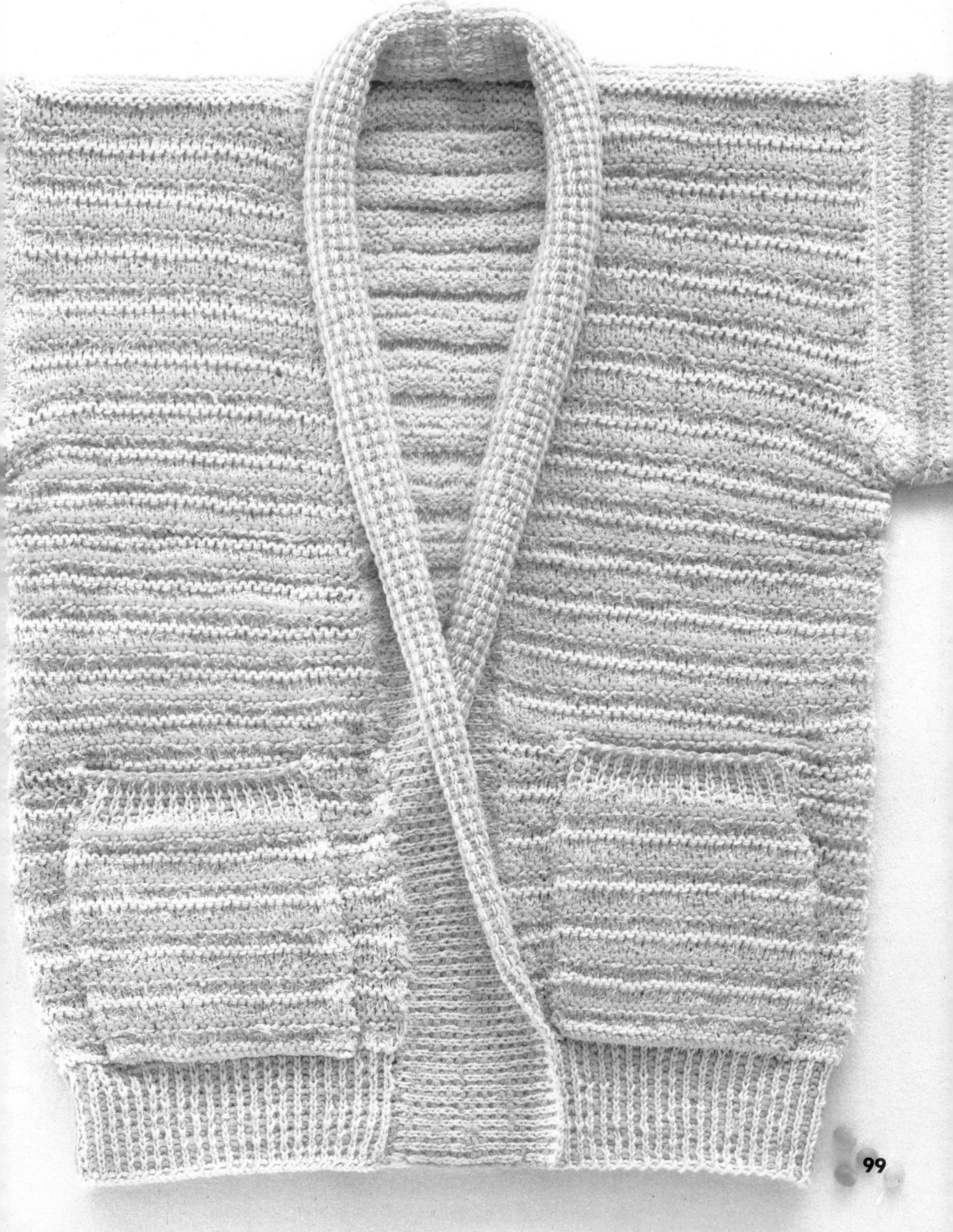

■ BELT LOOPS (Make 2)

Using larger needles and A, cast on 5 sts and work in rib as for back for 9cm. Cast off in rib using A only.

■ POCKETS (Make 2)

Using larger needles and A, cast on 36 sts and work in stripe patt for 14cm. Change to smaller needles and work in rib as for back for 3cm. Cast off in rib using A only.

■ MAKING UP

Press according to instructions on yarn label.
Sew in sleeves, joining cast off edge of sleeves to row ends and top of sleeve shaping to cast off sts on body.
Join side and sleeve seams.
Join back neck seam of border.
Sew on belt loops.
Sew on pockets.

LONG VERSION

■ BACK

Using larger needles and A, cast on 109 sts and work in stripe patt as for back of cardigan version until back measures 72cm, ending with a WS row.

Armhole and neck shaping
Work as for cardigan version.

■ LEFT FRONT

Using larger needles and A, cast on 45 sts and work in stripe patt until front measures 68cm, ending with a RS row.

Front edge shaping
Work as for cardigan version.

■ RIGHT FRONT

Work as for left front, reversing shapings.

■ SLEEVES (Make 2)

Work as for cardigan version.

■ NECK BORDER (Worked in 2 halves)

Join shoulder seams.
With RS facing and using smaller needles and A, pick up and K123 sts up right front and across half of back neck.
Work in rib as for back for 10cm, beg with a 2nd row.
Cast off in rib using A only.
Work 2nd half beg at back neck.

■ BELT, BELT LOOPS AND POCKETS

As cardigan version.

■ MAKING UP

As cardigan version.

100

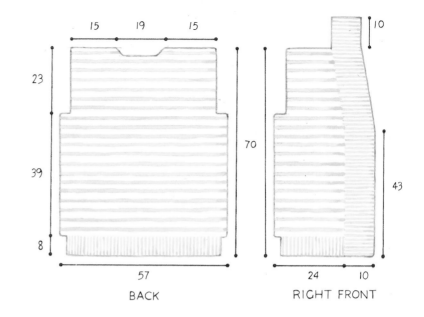

BACK

RIGHT FRONT

All measurements are in centimetres.

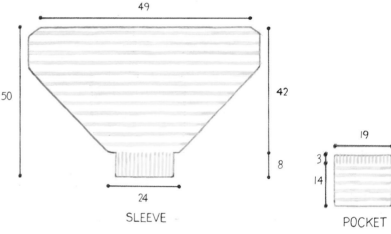

SLEEVE

POCKET

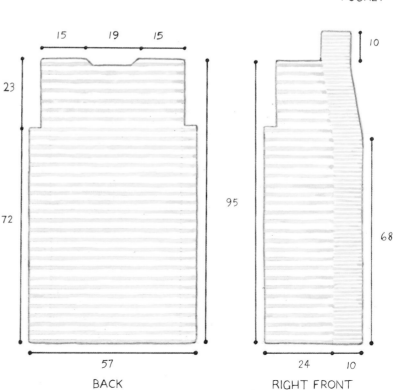

BACK

RIGHT FRONT

SUNSHINE

This textured design is made up of repeating patterns: leaves, an apple tree, an aqueduct and a cable stitch. The crispness of the cotton yarn give the intricate pattern a striking clarity.

■ SIZE

To fit 81-86[91-97:102-107]cm/32-34[36-38:40-42]in bust
Figures for larger sizes are given in square brackets. Where there is only one set of figures, this applies to all sizes.
See diagram for finished measurements.

■ MATERIALS

500[550:600]g fine mercerised cotton yarn
One pair each of 2¾mm and 3¼mm knitting needles *or size to obtain correct tension*
One cable needle

■ TENSION

28 sts and 32 rows to 10cm over st st using larger needles
Check your tension before beginning.

■ BACK AND FRONT (Both alike)

Using smaller needles, cast on 114[118:122] sts and work in rib as foll:
1st rib row (RS) K2, *P2, K2, rep from * to end.
2nd rib row P2, *K2, P2, rep from * to end.
Rep last 2 rib rows 16 times.
inc row K5, * M1, K2, rep from * to last 5 sts, M1, K5. 167[173:179] sts.
Change to larger needles and work in leaf patt as foll:
1st row (WS) K3, *K5, purl into back of st – called P1 tbl –, rep from * to last 2 sts, K2.
2nd row P2, *knit into back of st – called K1 tbl –, P5, rep from * to last 3 sts, P3.
3rd row As first row.
4th row As 2nd row.
5th row As first row.
6th row P2, *(K1, yfwd, K1) into next st, P5, rep from * to last 3 sts, P3.
7th row K3, *K5, P3, rep from * to last 2 sts, K2.
8th row P1, *(P1, K1) into next st, K1, yfwd, K1, yfwd, K1, P2tog, P2, rep from * to last 4 sts, P4.
9th row K2, *K5, P5, rep from * to last 3 sts, K3.
10th row *P2, (P1, K1) into next st, K2, yfwd, K1, yfwd, K2, P2tog, rep from * to last 5 sts, P5.
11th row K1, *K5, P7, rep from * to last 4 sts, K4.
12th row P3, *(P1, K1) into next st, K3, yfwd, K1, yfwd, K3, P2tog, P2, rep from * to last 2 sts, P2.
13th row K5, *P9, K5, rep from* to end.

14th row P4, *(P1, K1) into next st, slip next 2 sts one at a time k-wise, then insert point of LH needle into fronts of these 2 sts and knit them tog – called ssk –, K5, K2tog, P2tog, P2, rep from * to last st, P1.
15th row K4, * P7, K5, rep from * to last st, K1.
16th row P3, *P2, (P1, K1) into next st, ssk, K3, K2tog, P2tog, rep from * to last 2sts, P2.
17th row K3, *P5, K5, rep from * to last 2 sts, K2.
18th row P4, *P2, (P1, K1) into next st, ssk, K1, K2tog, P2tog, rep from * to last st, P1.
19th row K2, *P3, K5, rep from * to last 3 sts, K3.
20th row P4, *P4, sl 1, K2tog, psso, P1, rep from * to last st, P1.
21st row K.
22nd row P.
23rd row K.
24th row P, inc 3[1:1] sts evenly. 170[174:180] sts.
Now work apple tree patt as foll:
1st row (WS) K0[2:5], (K14, P6, K14) 5 times, K0[2:5].
2nd row K0[2:5], (P14, K6, P14) 5 times, K0[2:5].
Rep last 2 rows 5 times.
13th row As first row.
14th row K0[2:5], (P14, M1, K6, M1, P14) 5 times, K0[2:5].
15th row K0[2:5], (K14, P8, K14) 5 times, K0[2:5].
16th row K0[2:5], (P14, K1, M1, K6, M1, K1, P14) 5 times, K0[2:5].
17th row K0[2:5], (K14, P10, K14) 5 times, K0[2:5].
18th row K0[2:5], (P12, slip next 2 sts onto cable needle and leave at back of work, K2, then P2 from cable needle – called TB4 –, K6, slip next 2 sts onto cable needle and leave at front of work, P2, then K2 from cable needle – called TF4 –, P12) 5 times, K0[2:5].
19th row K0[2:5], (K12, P2, K2, P6, K2, P2, K12) 5 times, K0[2:5].

20th row K0[2:5], (P10, TB4, P2, M1, K6, M1, P2, TF4, P10) 5 times, K0[2:5].
21st row K0[2:5], (K10, P2, K4, P8, K4, P2, K10) 5 times, K0[2:5].
22nd row K0[2:5], (P8, TB4, P4, K1, M1, K6, M1, K1, P4, TF4, P8) 5 times, K0[2:5].
23rd row K0[2:5], (K8, P2, K6, P10, K6, P2, K8) 5 times, K0[2:5].
24th row K0[2:5], (P6, TB4, P4, TB4, K6, TF4, P4, TF4, P6) 5 times, K0[2:5].
25th row K0[2:5], (K6, P2, K6, P2, K2, P6, K2, P2, K6, P2, K6) 5 times, K0[2:5].
26th row K0[2:5], (P6, K2, P4, TB4, P2, K6, P2, TF4, P4, K2, P6) 5 times, K0[2:5].
27th row K0[2:5], (K6, [P2, K4] twice, P6, [K4, P2] twice, K6) 5 times, K0[2:5].
28th row K0[2:5], (P5, K into 2nd st, P first st, slip both sts from needle – called TB2 –, K1B, P2, TB4, P4, K6, P4, TF4, P2, K1 tbl, P into back of 2nd st, K first st, slip both sts from needle – called TF2 –, P5) 5 times, K0[2:5].
29th row K0[2:5], (K5, P1, K1, P1, K2, P2, K6, P6, K6, P2, K2, P1, K1, P1, K5) 5 times, K0[2:5].
30th row K0[2:5], (P4, TB2, P1, [K1, P1, K1, P1, K1] into next st, turn, K5, turn, P5, turn, K2tog, K1, K2tog, turn, sl 1, K2tog, psso – called make bobble or MB –, P2, K2, P4, TB4, K2, TF4, P4, K2, P2, MB, P1, TF2, P4) 5 times, K0[2:5].
31st row K0[2:5], (K2tog, K2, P1, K5, P2, K4 [P2, K2] twice, P2, K4, P2, K5, P1, K2, K2tog) 5 times, K0[2:5].
32nd row K0[2:5], (P2, TB2, P4, TB2, K1 tbl, P2, TB4, P2, K2, P2, TF4, P2, K1 tbl, TF2, P4, TF2, P2) 5 times, K0[2:5].
33rd row K0[2:5], (K2, P1, K5, P1, K1, P1, K2, P2, K4, P2, K4, P2, K2, P1, K1, P1, K5, P1, K2) 5 times, K0[2:5].
34th row K0[2:5], (P2, MB, P4, TB2, P1, MB, P2, K2, P4, K2, P4, K2, P2, MB, P1, TF2, P4, MB, P2) 5 times, K0[2:5].
35th row K0[2:5], (K2tog, K5, P1, K5, [P2, K4] twice, P2, K5, P1, K5, K2tog) 5 times, K0[2:5].
36th row K0[2:5], (P5, TB2, P4, TB2, K1 tbl, P4, K2, P4, K1 tbl, TF2, P4, TF2, P5) 5 times, K0[2:5].
37th row K0[2:5], ([K5, P1] twice, K1, P1, K4, P2, K4, P1, K1, [P1, K5] twice) 5 times, K0[2:5].

All measurements are in centimetres.

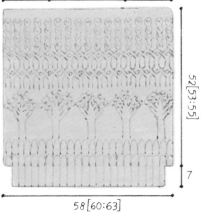

FRONT/BACK

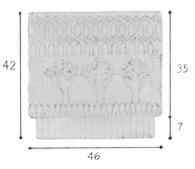

SLEEVE

38th row K0[2:5], (P5, MB, P4, TB2, P1, MB, P3, TB2, TF2, P3, MB, P1, TF2, P4, MB, P5) 5 times, K0[2:5].
39th row K0[2:5], (K2tog, K8, P1, K6, P1, K2, P1, K6, P1, K8, K2tog) 5 times, K0[2:5].
40th row K0[2:5], (P8, TB2, P5, TB2, P2, TF2, P5, TF2, P8) 5 times, K0[2:5].
41st row K0[2:5], (K8, P1, K6, P1, K4, P1, K6, P1, K8) 5 times, K0[2:5].
42nd row K0[2:5], (P8, MB, P5, TB2, P4, TF2, P5, MB, P8) 5 times, K0[2,5].
43rd row K0[2:5], (K2tog, K12, P1, K6, P1, K12, K2tog) 5 times, K0[2:5].
44th row K0[2:5], (P13, MB, P6, MB, P13) 5 times, K0[2:5].
45th row K.
46th row P.
Rep last 2 rows twice.
First size only:
Next row K2tog, K31, (K2tog, K32) 3 times, K2tog, K31, K2tog. 164 sts.
2nd size only:
Next row K86, K2tog, K86. 173 sts.
3rd size only:
Next row (K1, P1) into first st, K to last st, (K1, P1) into last st. 182 sts.
All sizes:
Now work aqueduct patt as foll:
1st row (RS) P2, *P3, (K1 tbl, K1) into next st, then insert LH needle point behind the vertical strand that runs downward from between the 2 sts just made, and K1 tbl into this strand to make 3 sts from one – called inc 2 –, P5, rep from * to end.
2nd row *K5, P3, K3, rep from * to last 2 sts, K2.
3rd row P2, *P3, K1, sl 1, K1, P5, rep from * to end.
Rep last 2 rows 3 times.
10th row As 2nd row.
11th row P2, *P3, K1, inc 2, K1, P5, rep from * to end.
12th row K5, P2, K1, P2, *K8, P2, K1, P2, rep from * to last 5 sts, K5.
13th row P2, *P2, slip one st onto cable needle and leave at back of work, K2, then K1 from cable needle – called BKC –, P1, slip 2 sts onto cable needle and leave at front of work, K1, then K2 from cable needle – called FKC –, P4, rep from * to end.
14th row K4, P2, P1 tbl, K1, P1 tbl, P2, K1, *K5, P2, P1 tbl, K1, P1 tbl, P2, K1, rep from * to last 3 sts, K3.
15th row *P3, slip one st onto cable needle and leave at back of work, K2, then P1 from cable needle – called BPC –, K1 tbl, P1, K1 tbl, slip 2 sts onto cable needle and leave at front of work, P1, then K2 from cable needle – called FPC –, P1, rep from * to last 2 sts, P2.
16th row *K3, P2, [K1, P1 tbl] twice, K1, P2, K1, rep from * to last 2 sts, K2.
17th row P1, * slip 2 sts onto cable needle and leave at back of work, K2, then K2 from cable needle – called BC4 –, (P1, K1 tbl) twice, P1, slip 2 sts

onto cable needle and leave at front of work, K2, then K2 from cable needle – called FC4 –, rep from * to last st, P1.
18th row K1, *P2, (K1, PB1) 4 times, K1, P2, rep from * to last st, K1.
19th row P1, K2, *(P1, K1 tbl) 4 times, P1, FC4, rep from * to last 12 sts, (P1, K1 tbl) 4 times, P1, K2, P1.

20th row K1, *P2, (K1, P1 tbl) 4 times, K1, P2, rep from * to last st, K1.
21st row P1, *TF4, (P1, K1 tbl) twice, P1, TB4, rep from * to last st, P1.
22nd row K2, *K1, P2, (K1, P1 tbl) twice, K1, P2, K3, rep from * to end.
23rd row P2, *P1, TF4, P1, TB4, P3, rep from * to end.
24th row *K5, ssk, K3tog, pass ssk over the K3tog – called dec 5 –, K3, rep from * to last 2 sts, K2.
These 24 rows form aqueduct patt.
Rep patt once more.
Work 4 rows in rev st st.
Back should now measure approx 49cm.
Next row P2tog, P to last 2 sts, P2tog. 162[171:180] sts.
Now work in cable patt as foll:
1st row (WS) *K2, P1, K3, P1, K2, rep from * to end.
2nd row *P2, K1, P3, K1, P2, rep from * to end.
3rd row As first row.
4th row *P2, K1, P1, MB, P1, K1, P2, rep from * to end.
5th row As first row.
6th row As 2nd row.
7th row As first row.
8th row *P2, yarn to back of work between 2 needles – called yb –, sl 1, yarn to front of work between 2 needles – called yfwd –, P3, yb, sl 1, yfwd, P2, rep from * to end.
9th row K2, yfwd, sl 1, yb, K3, yfwd, sl 1, yb, K2, rep from * to end.
10th row P2, slip 4 sts onto cable

needle and leave at back of work, K1, then K4 from cable needle – called T5 –, P2, rep from * to end.
11th row *K2, P1, K3, P1, K2, rep from * to end.
12th row *P2, K1, P3, K1, P2, rep from * to end.
These 12 rows form cable patt.

Rep these 12 rows until back measures 57[58:60]cm, ending with a WS row.
Work 6 rows in moss st.
Cast off very loosely.

■ **SLEEVES** (Make 2)
Using smaller needles, cast on 62 sts and work 28 rows in rib as for back, ending with a 2nd row.
Inc row (K1, P1, K1) into first st, *M1, K1, rep from * to end. 125 sts.
Change to larger needles and work rows 1 to 21 of leaf patt.
Next row (K1, P1) into first st, P to end. 126 sts.
Work rows 1 to 44 of apple patt, but knit 12 extra sts at each side instead of 0[2:5].
Next row (P1, K1) into first st, K to last st, (K1, P1) into last st. 128 sts.
Work rows 1 to 24 of aqueduct patt twice.
Sleeve should measure approx 42cm.
Cast off very loosely.

■ **MAKING UP**
Join shoulder seams, leaving 26cm open for neck.
Place marker 23cm down from shoulder seam on back and front, and sew cast off edge of sleeve between markers.
Join side and sleeve seams.

HOT SHOT

Easy to knit and fun to wear, this simple short top is knitted up in cotton tape. The depth of the V at the back can be adjusted by simply altering the position of the buttons.

■ SIZE

One size to fit up to 97cm/38in bust
See diagram for finished measurements.

■ MATERIALS

300g cotton tape 10mm wide
One pair each of 7½mm and 10mm knitting needles *or size to obtain correct tension*
One 4.00mm crochet hook
Two 38mm buttons

■ TENSION

11 sts and 15 rows to 10cm over g st using larger needles
Check your tension before beginning.

■ FRONT

Using smaller needles, cast on 46 sts and work 2 rows in g st.
Change to larger needles and continue in g st, inc one st at each end of 12th and every foll 14th row 5 times in all. 56 sts.
Cast off.

■ LEFT BACK

Using smaller needles, cast on 30 sts and work 2 rows in g st.
Change to larger needles and cont in g st, shaping sides by dec one st at end of 2nd and every 4th row *and at the same time* inc one st at beg of 12th and every 14th row until back measures same as front. 18 sts.
Cast off.

■ RIGHT BACK

Work as for left back, reversing shapings and working buttonholes on 6th row from cast on edge as foll:
1st buttonhole row K3, cast off next 2 sts, K5, cast off next 2 sts, K to end.
2nd buttonhole row K, casting on 2 sts over those cast off on previous row.

■ MAKING UP

Join shoulder seams.
Join side seams leaving 18cm for armhole.
Using crochet hook, work one row of dc around armholes, up right back, around front neck and down left back to prevent stretching.
Sew on buttons.

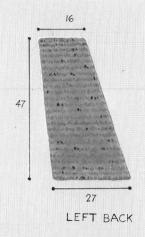

16

47

27

LEFT BACK

51

47

42

FRONT

All measurements are in centimetres.

SNAKES & LADDERS

The bold, broad-shouldered shape has an individual motif of snakes and ladders. You might want to try the noughts and crosses featured overleaf or leave the motifs off altogether.

■ SIZE
One size to fit up to 102cm/40in bust
See diagram for finished measurements.

■ MATERIALS
Use a lightweight cotton yarn and cotton slub.
450g slub yarn main colour A (white)
450g slub yarn main colour B (black)
25g contrast cotton yarn C (pink)
One pair of 3mm knitting needles
One circular 5mm knitting needle 80cm long *or size to obtain correct tension*
Two shoulder pads

■ TENSION
17 sts and 25 rows to 10cm over st st using larger needles
Check your tension before beginning.

Note
Read chart from right to left for RS knit rows and left to right for WS purl rows.

Unless stated st st is used throughout. Use separate balls of yarn for each area, do not carry yarn across back of work. Take care to twist yarns at back when changing colours to avoid holes forming (see page 114). The rib of the body is included in the chart.

■ FRONT
Using smaller needles, cast on 100 sts using A and B alternately as on chart. Work from row 1 of chart in K1, P1 rib for 3cm.
Change to larger needle and cont without shaping to end of row 80.

Sleeve shaping
Inc one st at each end of next and foll 5th row. 104 sts.
Work 4 rows without shaping.
Inc one st at each end of next and foll 3rd row. 108 sts.
Work 2 rows without shaping.

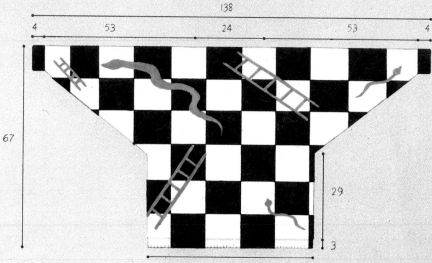

FRONT/BACK

All measurements are in centimetres.

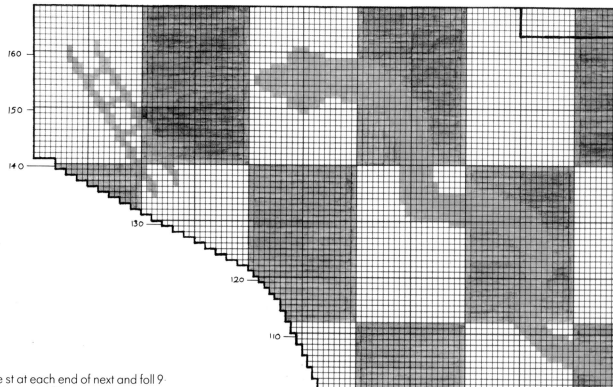

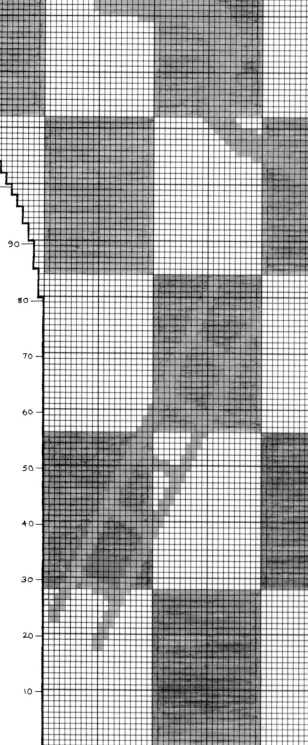

Inc one st at each end of next and foll 9
alternate rows. 128 sts.
Inc one st at each end of next 6 rows.
140 sts.
Inc 2 sts (by working 3 times into st) at
each end of next 18 rows. 212 sts.
Cast on 4 sts at beg of next 2 rows. 220
sts.
Cont without shaping until end of row
164.
Next row Work 90 sts in st st, work
centre 40 sts in K1, P1 rib, work in st st
to end.
Rep last row twice.
Next row Patt 90 sts, cast off centre 40
sts in rib, patt to end.
Leave rem sts on a spare needle.

BACK
Work as for front, working mirror
image by reversing order of colours
and working checks only (omitting
snakes and ladders).
Join shoulders as foll:
Place front and back together with
right sides facing and using a 3rd
needle, K through back and front and
cast off.
Cast off rem shoulder as first.

CUFFS (Make 2)
With RS facing and using smaller
needles pick up and K40 sts evenly
along sleeve edge using B for front of
wrist and A for back wrist.
Work 4cm in K1, P1 rib.
Cast off loosely in rib.

MAKING UP
Join underarm and side seams. Press
garment according to instructions on
yarn label.
Insert shoulder pads.

108

FRONT

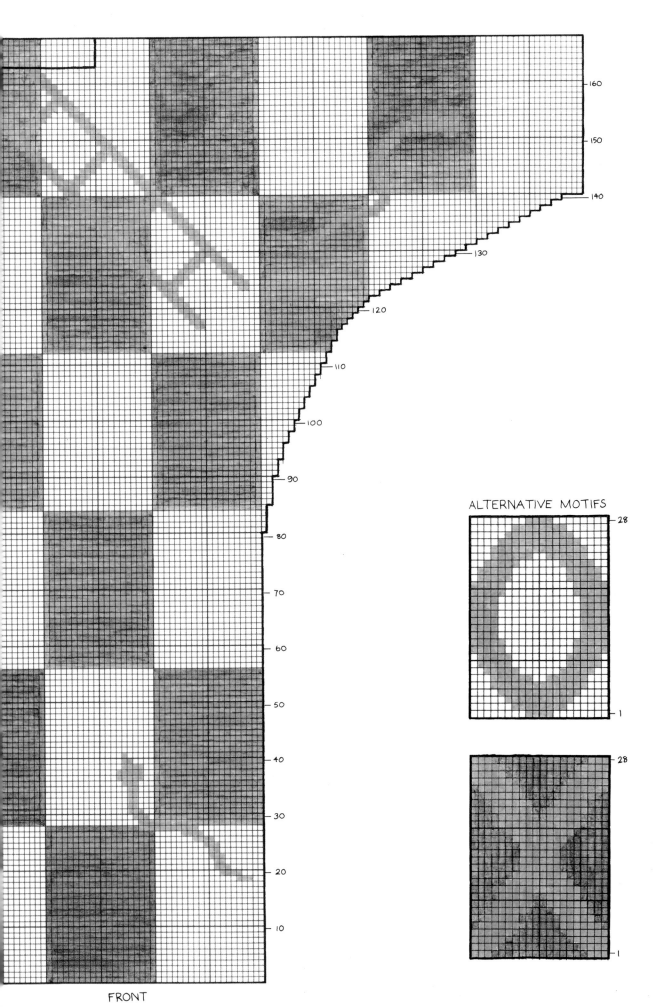

ALTERNATIVE MOTIFS

160

150

140

130

120

110

100

90

80

70

60

50

40

30

20

10

FRONT

28

1

28

1

109

TENSION & MEASUREMENTS

On the following nine pages, we concentrate on useful hints for good knitting and how to achieve a professional finish with cotton. We are assuming that the reader already has a good knowledge of basic knitting techniques. A right-handed knitter is shown in the illustrations. If you are left-handed, prop the book up in front of a mirror: you can then interpret the method without difficulty. Some of the designers in this book specify certain techniques and finishes in their instructions; others do not. You can choose from those illustrated here.

■ NEEDLE SIZES

English	000	00	0	1	2	3	4	5	6	7	8	9	10	11	12	13	14
Metric	10	9	8	7½	7	6½	6	5½	5	4½	4	3¾	3¼	3	2¾	2¼	2
American	15	13	11	–	–	10½	10	9	8	7	6	5	4	3	2	1	0

■ TENSION

The tension of your knitting is determined by the type of yarn used, how thick or thin it is, the size of needles and the amount of yarn pulled through for every stitch, which varies from knitter to knitter and with beginners is not usually consistent. The two samples of knitting pictured below illustrate the difference a change in needle size makes. They are both by

the same knitter, using the same yarn but on needles .5mm different in size. Note how different the fabrics look.

The tension or stitch gauge of a garment is given at the beginning of every pattern. It specifies the number of stitches and rows over a 10cm square on the designer's knitted fabric. If your knitting cannot match this stitch gauge, the fit and shape of your finished garment will not correspond to the illustrated design and measurement diagram. There is a risk that the garment might change drastically in length or width and your work will be spoiled.

■ MAKING A TENSION SQUARE

Before starting to knit any design, you need to make a tension square. Work with the size of needles and the yarn type and weight stated in the pattern. Knit the main pattern stitches of the garment for a square measuring about 12cm and cast off. It is important to reproduce the main pattern exactly because this will influence the tension. Any cables or colour changes should be included, for example.

Lay the square out flat (do not press first) and measure the number of rows

per 10cm and the number of stitches per 10cm. Having taken this reading, wash, dry and press the square and measure it again to make sure that washing doesn't alter the tension. (Cotton sometimes 'bulks up' when washed and it might not return to the original tension.)

If your tension reading is different to that specified in the pattern, the simplest way to rectify this is by using a different size needle. To obtain fewer stitches and rows per 10cm, use a larger needle, and to obtain more, use a finer needle until you have the correct tension for the pattern. Even if your tension is only slightly different, this difference will be increased over the whole garment.

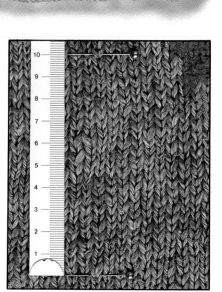

110

■ READING CHARTS

Each square of the charts in this book represents a stitch and each line corresponds to a row of knitting. The colour changes are indicated on each square of the chart.

To knit from a chart read from the right hand corner to the left for the right side of your design, and from left to right of the chart for the wrong side. To make it easier to keep track of the pattern, place a ruler under each row as you knit it. If you want to substitute a different motif or your own design on a sweater, this is easily done by transferring a charted or squared design (say from a source such as cross stitch embroidery or canvas work), which you then draw freehand onto a chart within the outline of your sweater, or onto graph paper. It is important to understand that although the chart is marked in squares, stitches themselves are not square. They are usually wider than they are long, so a successful design may appear slightly longer on the chart in proportion to the width than it will appear on the finished garment.

If you are working with a chart which doesn't show the outline of the whole garment but represents only a small, repeated section, such as fair isle (see page 18), and you need to increase for shaping, any increases must be incorporated into new repeats of the pattern.

The chart on the left is shown knitted up below.

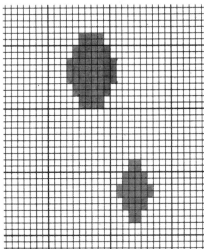

■ MEASUREMENTS

Knitting designs have varying amounts of ease written into the pattern instructions. A jacket, for example, will have a deeper armhole than a sweater so that there is plenty of room for other clothes underneath it; a loose T-shirt design will measure far more around the bust than the actual body measurement; a tight rib will be constructed so that it stretches when worn and shrinks back when taken off.

The measurement diagrams with each pattern in this book include ease and are not measurements that relate directly to body measurements. It is important for you to decide at the outset whether you want the garment to be figure-hugging or loose-fitting.

To ensure a baggier sizing, knit up a garment that measures at least 10cm more than your actual bust measurement. In some designs, only one size is given to fit up to a certain bust size. To calculate your size and fashion requirements, the body measurements you should record are:

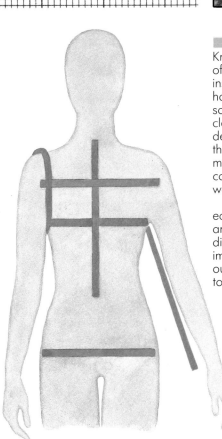

ABBREVIATIONS

approx	approximately
beg	begin(ning)
cm	centimetre(s)
cont	continu(e)(ing)
dec	decreas(e)(ing)
dc	double crochet
foll	follow(s)(ing)
g st	garter stitch
g	gram(s)
in	inch(es)
inc	increas(e)(ing)
K	knit
k-wise	knitwise
LH	left hand (needle)
mm	millimetre(s)
psso	pass slip stitch(es) over
patt	pattern
P	purl
p-wise	purlwise
rem	remain(s)(ing)
rep	repeat(ing)
rev st st	reverse stocking stitch
RH	right hand (needle)
RS	right side
sl	slip
st(s)	stitch(es)
st st	stocking stitch
tbl	through back of loop(s)
tog	together
WS	wrong side
yb	yarn to back of work
yon	yarn over needle
yrn	yarn around needle
yfwd	yarn forward
M1	make one st by picking up horizontal loop lying before next st and working into the back of it.
*	repeat instructions following or between *
( )	repeat instructions inside brackets

Any other abbreviations are explained in the text for each design.

1 Bust, around fullest part of bust.
2 Back length, nape of neck to waist or where garment should extend to.
3 Shoulder width, across back at shoulder blades.
4 Underarm, from armpit to where finished garment should end.
5 Hip, at the widest part.
6 Armhole.
Check these measurements, where appropriate, against the measurement diagram and calculate which size you want to knit up.

BASIC TECHNIQUES

■ CASTING ON

Casting on forms the first row of loops of the knitted fabric. It is important that the stitches are of an even size to produce a neat edge. Different casting on methods are suitable for particular types of finish. Some garments require

an elastic edge, others a firm edge or even an invisible edge. The relative elasticity of cotton requires a firmer edge than other types of yarn.

If you want to add a hem or the rib band onto the sleeve or body of the garment afterwards, cast on in the

usual way and knit up the body of the garment. When you have finished the knitting, use a knitting needle to pick up and knit the loops from the cast on edge on the right side of the garment. These will become the first row of knitting for the hem or rib band. This is particularly useful if the rib stretches with washing and wearing – you can then unpick the rib and redo it.

■ SLIP LOOP

The slip loop is the first stitch to cast on. Wind a length of yarn around two fingers and then a second time, taking the yarn to the back of the first loop,

away from you (1). Using either a needle or your other hand, bring the second loop through the first loop (2) and by pulling the two ends of yarn,

tighten the loop on the needle (3). The remaining stitches can be cast on using your usual method – either with two needles or your thumb.

■ CABLE CAST ON

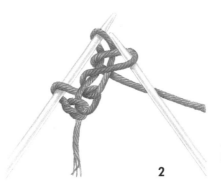
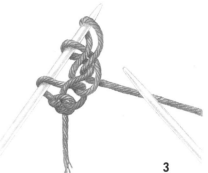

This gives an elastic and decorative edge. This method is worked with two needles. Start with a slip loop, cast on one more stitch by knitting into the slip loop and slipping the new stitch back

onto the left-hand needle. Insert the right-hand needle *between* the slip loop and the new cast on stitch (1). Take the yarn around the needle and pull through a new stitch (2) and slip

the new stitch back onto the left-hand needle (3). If you want to emphasize the rope-like edge that the cable cast on creates, use two strands of yarn for the cast on row.

■ INVISIBLE CAST ON

This cast on method gives a single ribbed edge that looks very professional, almost like a machine-

knitted edge. It is ideal for cardigans and waistcoats.

You will need a length of contrast yarn. With the length of contrast yarn

make a slip loop and cast on half the number of stitches specified in the pattern you have chosen to knit up plus one extra stitch. Now change to your chosen yarn and follow this pattern for the first 6 rows (1), then revert to the master pattern for the required length of rib.

1st row K1, *yfwd, K1, rep from * to end.
2nd row K1, *yarn to front of work between needles (yft), sl 1, yarn to back of work between needles (yb), K1, rep from * to end.
3rd row Sl 1, *yb, K1, yft, sl 1, rep from * to end.
4th row As 2nd row.
5th row As 3rd row.
6th row K1, *P1, K1, rep from * to end. Remove contrast yarn (2).

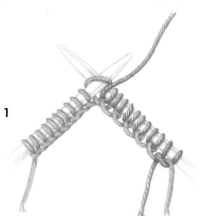
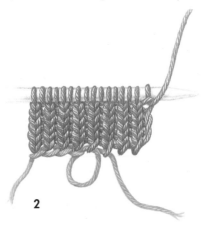

EDGES

Tension is just as important on the edges of your knitting as on the main body of the garment.

To make a firm cast on edge, knit into the back of the stitches on the first row (except when you cable cast on when you knit into the front).

When casting off, use the same stitches as those you have been working over the pattern.

The left and right edges of a garment (known as selvedges) can be decorative where they will show but must be firm where they are enclosed for a neat seam. Decorative selvedges

are worked over two stitches each side to prevent the fabric from curling. The second and next to last stitch on every knit row are purled.

Selvedges to be seamed or where stitches will be picked up later are worked over one stitch on each side as shown below.

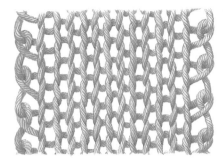

The most common method of working the selvedge is merely to knit all stitches on knit rows and purl them on purl rows.

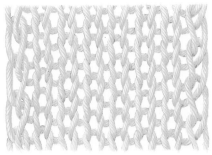

To make a chain edge, slip the first and last stitch of every knit row knitwise. Purl all stitches on the purl row.

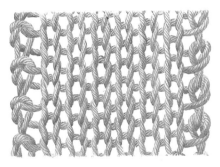

The slip stitch edge forms a neat base for picking up stitches. Slip the first stitch of every row knitwise and knit the last stitch of every row.

CROCHET CAST OFF

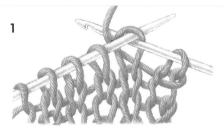

1

The crochet cast off is a good method to use with cotton as it is less likely to produce too tight an edge. Using a crochet hook, knit the first stitch. Take

2

the yarn to the back of the work and insert the crochet hook through the front of the next stitch (1). With the crochet hook, draw the yarn through

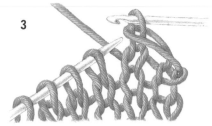

3

the second and first stitches (2). Retain this stitch on the hook (3) and repeat the process until all stitches have been cast off.

INVISIBLE CAST OFF

The invisible cast off method is used when further knitting is to be added later on. Cut the main yarn, leaving a length longer than the width of the main knitting. Thread the yarn through a blunt-ended needle and draw it through the stitches on the last row of knitting. Secure the yarn by knotting through the last loop. When you come to complete the garment, pick up the stitches, withdraw the threaded yarn and rejoin a new ball of yarn.

CIRCULAR KNITTING

In circular knitting the work progresses in rounds, producing a tubular fabric with only two edges – top and bottom. Tubular fabric can be knitted on three or more double pointed needles with an extra needle for the knitting itself. One circular needle with rigid points at each end and a flexible length between them is particularly suitable for sleeves or a large piece of work.

A round is complete when all the stitches have been knitted back to the first cast on stitch. To close the circle, knit into the first cast on stitch, which will be marked by the free end of yarn. All rounds, colour changes and pattern changes begin and end at this point.

When working with several needles, it may be easier to cast on all the stitches onto one needle and then divide the stitches equally between the number of needles you are using. Make sure the same number of stitches is kept on each needle while knitting.

Some of the designs in this book are knitted in one piece to the armholes or the body and sleeves are knitted in one piece. A flexible circular needle is very useful when trying to manage such a large number of stitches and such a weight of fabric. However, if you are knitting a cardigan, for example, you must turn the work and knit back and forth in rows even though you are using a circular needle. Once you become accustomed to using circular needles, you may find them easier for all your knitting.

ELASTIC IN RIBS

A useful technique for ensuring a firm, fitting ribbed band is to knit in shirring elastic across the back of the rib. Twist the elastic around the main yarn every two stitches of knitting and on every row, making sure you maintain the correct tension; don't pull the elastic tight. To elasticate a ribbed band at the end of knitting see page 118.

113

JOINING IN YARN

Many of the designs in this book have used more than one coloured yarn. Joining in a new colour and working the yarn, when not in use, into the back of the fabric are techniques that need to be mastered if the garment is to look good and wear well.

You must be careful to choose the method most appropriate to the yarn and the garment. For example, if you make a cotton summer top and weave the yarn not in use across the back of the work, the top may become heavy because of the strands of extra yarn and too warm for your purposes. Alternatively, if you strand yarns across too many stitches, the loose strands may catch on jewellery and ruin the garment.

Unless you are creating an isolated area of colour, it is never advisable to join yarn in the middle of a row. It has a tendency to distort the stitches where it is joined. Always make sure you have sufficient yarn to finish a row and then join a new ball or colour at the side edge.

Work the first few stitches with the new yarn. Tie the old yarn to the new to secure it until you make the garment up and darn in all the loose ends. Alternatively, you can knit in the loose ends as you go to save time later.

It should only be necessary to join a new ball of yarn in the middle of a row if you are working on an isolated area of colour. Work the first stitch with the new yarn leaving long enough loose ends to darn in later. Always remember to cross the two colours over to prevent a hole forming – a technique known as intarsia.

When joining yarn in the middle of a row, it is tidier to knit the loose end of the new yarn into the work as you go. This cuts down on the time you need to make up and finish the garment.

■ INTARSIA

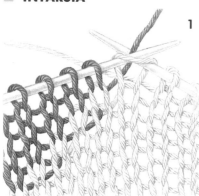 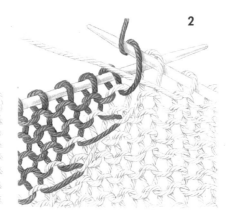

This method is also known as crossing colours – every colour being worked has its own ball of yarn for each area. This is used when isolated areas of colour appear on the fabric or when the same colours occur at some distance from each other. Yarns are crossed over at the join with the neighbouring colour so that no hole forms. If you are using a large number of colours over small areas, it is easiest to use lengths of yarn or bobbins of yarn instead of balls to avoid tangling.

On a knit row (1), take the new yarn over the old yarn and drop the old yarn to the back of the work. Continue knitting with the new colour.

On a purl row (2), cross the new yarn over the old yarn in the same way.

Intarsia fabrics are very tidy with few loose ends and they can often look virtually the same on both sides.

■ COLOUR INSERTIONS

One way of inserting blocks of contrast colour is with a technique called 'short rows' or 'turning'. The method involves knitting across a certain number of stitches (as specified in the pattern), turning the work and leaving the remaining stitches unworked until the colour insertion is completed. At the beginning of every 'short' or 'turned' row, the first stitch is slipped and the next worked tightly to prevent a hole forming. When the insertion is completed, pick up and knit across the remaining stitches. Because this type of insertion creates extra rows of knitting, the colour shapes are usually staggered across the work to compensate (see page 50).

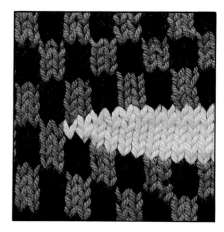

This strip of inserted colour is worked using only one ball of yarn at a time.

STRANDING

It is very important to maintain the correct tension when using this technique. It is easy to pull the floating yarns at the back of the work too tight and this causes the fabric to pucker. Check your tension as you work by flattening out the knitting to see if there are any tight areas. Stranding does

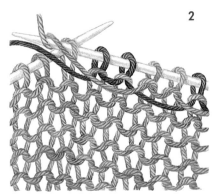

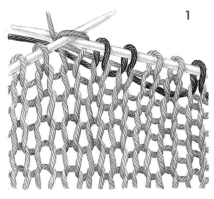

The wrong side shows the neat strands of the two colours in this checked garment.

restrict the stretch of a garment. It is not advisable to strand the yarn over more than five stitches in a row as the loops will catch and distort the garment or break off and create holes.

When stranding the yarn on a knit row (1), knit the required number of stitches in the main colour and drop the yarn to the back of the work. Knit the next stitches in the contrast colour and drop the contrast yarn to the back of the work. Repeat in this way,

allowing the unused yarn to float across the back of the work. If you pull the first stitch in a new colour too tightly, you will pucker the work. When stranding on a purl row (2), bring the yarns to the front of the work and work as for a knit row, but keeping the floating yarns at the front. With practice, you will find you can build up speed by using your index finger for one colour and another finger for the other colour.

WEAVING IN

This is the method used for designs with frequent large repeats where five or more stitches separate a colour repeat, or where several colours have to be worked in one row. It is important to avoid long floats across the back of the work. These catch, causing holes and distortions. By weaving in, you can produce a well-finished fabric but the more colours you carry across the back of the work, the thicker and warmer the fabric will be. If there are only a couple of repeats and they are far apart, it might be sensible to cross the colours (intarsia) and use separate balls of yarn for each area. It is also very important to keep to your correct tension when weaving in. Looser rather than tighter weaving in is advisable. Check that the woven-in yarns are not showing through the work.

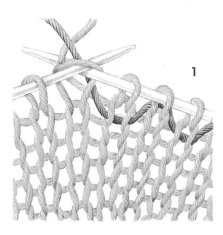

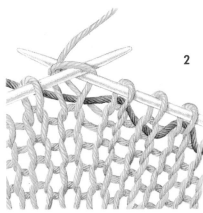

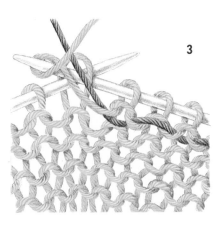

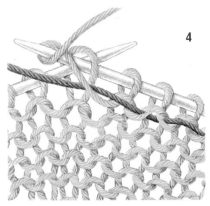

The reverse side of the work should look as though the yarn has been threaded through the back of the work.

When weaving in on a knit row, hold the main yarn as you would normally and the contrast with the forefinger of your other hand. Knit one stitch with the main yarn, feeding the contrast over the stitch as you work (1). Knit the next stitch over the contrast (2). When

weaving the yarn across the work on a purl row, work as for a knit row but keep the yarns at the front of the work. Feed the contrast over the main yarn and work one stitch (3), then purl the next stitch keeping the contrast below the main yarn (4).

115

▨ RIB DESIGNS

So often the use of multi-coloured patterns is restricted to the body of the garment and sometimes the sleeves. Some of the designs in this book have the colour scheme extended into the rib band too.

Top left: *A simple method of introducing colour into the ribbed bands of the body of the garment and the sleeves is to cast on in a contrast yarn. This is particularly effective if the contrast is used again in the design as for example on Tiger tails (see page 81).*

Top right: *The Balloons sweater (see page 34) has horizontal stripes of the contrast colours across the rib.*

Bottom left: *The two main colours of the design have been worked for the purl and knit stitches in the rib on the Chequerboard cardigan (see page 61).*

Bottom right: *Some bands are worked in a long narrow strip and sewn onto the body of the garment when it is made up. This method has been used on Zigzag (see page 22); the colours were worked in rows of knit and purl to imitate the ribbed effect. It is easier to work striped bands in this way.*

FINISHING & MAKING UP

However beautifully a garment has been knitted, unless time and care are taken over the making up and finishing stages, the garment will look unattractive and the effort spent on the actual knitting will have been wasted.

▨ JOINING SEAMS

Certain seam finishes are more appropriate to the weight of yarn or to the garment. Sometimes the seam can be used as a decorative feature.

Edge to edge seam (1)
This achieves an almost invisible edge and is useful for ribbed bands and cuffs. As they will be visible, the selvedges to be joined must be neat and have an equal number of rows.

Butt the pieces to be joined up against each other on the wrong side. Using a blunt-ended needle to avoid splitting the stitches, thread with a length of matching yarn. Work from side to side, taking the needle through the edge stitch on both sides. Continue this stitch along the length of the seam.

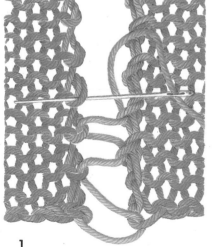

1

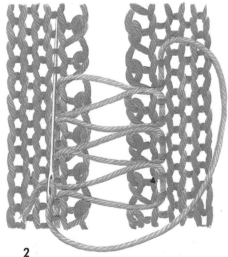

2

Mattress stitch (2)
This is a neat seam which is worked from the right side. With right sides uppermost, on a flat surface, butt both pieces to be joined edge to edge. Insert the threaded blunt-ended

needle through the two bar loops next to the selvedge stitch and take the needle across to the other edge. Continue working from side to side for the whole seam. The selvedge itself will be hidden by the oversewing.

3

4

Backstitch seam (3)
This is a common method for strong seams. Place the right sides of the pieces to be joined together, matching the rows and pattern repeats. With a threaded blunt-ended needle, work in backstitch as close to the edge as possible. The stitches must be small to ensure there are no gaps left along the seam but do not pull the seam too tight or there will be very little 'give'.

Decorative raised seam (4)
This makes a neat shoulder seam. To achieve this finish, cast off on the right side of the work. Place the wrong sides of the pieces to be joined together. With a threaded blunt-ended needle, pick up the outside of the cast off stitch on one piece and take the needle across to the other cast off edge. Work from side to side to the end of the seam.

Neat, even stitches make this decorative seam a feature of the finishing on this mercerised cotton cardigan (see page 39).

JOINING WITH NEEDLES
Casting off together is a method of joining two pieces of work while the stitches are still on the needles. The two pieces to be joined (most commonly at the shoulder seam) must have the same number of stitches. The finished seam forms a ridge and is visible on the right side of the garment.

Do not cast off the shoulder edge stitches, and finish knitting on a wrong side row. There should be the same number of stitches on both needles.

With the knitting needles parallel, and with the wrong sides of the work together, take a third needle and knit the first stitch on both needles together

1

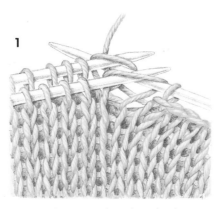

2

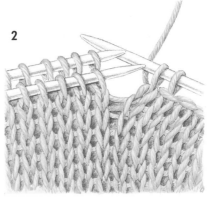

(1). Knit the second stitch on both needles together (2) and cast the first stitch off over the second.

Continue casting off in this way until only one stitch remains. Fasten off securely.

HEMMING
In place of a ribbed band, make a hem to give a flat, professional finish that won't curl up. Work an extra number of rows for the desired depth of the hem. Cast off loosely in the normal way. Turn the hem down and slipstitch the cast off edge to the garment.

There is another method of hemming in which you do not cast off as usual but finish work on a right side row. Leave the stitches on the knitting needle. Thread a blunt-ended needle with the main yarn and with the wrong side facing you, take the yarn through the first stitch on the knitting needle, slip it off, then pick up a stitch on the row of the garment to which the hem is to be attached. Continue until all the stitches are sewn down.

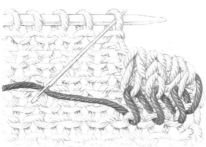

The edge of this shawl collar has been neatly hemmed (see page 47). If you hem any other edge of a garment, such as the bottom of a ribless T-shirt, remember that the hem will produce a bulkier fabric which may accentuate your waist or hip measurements.

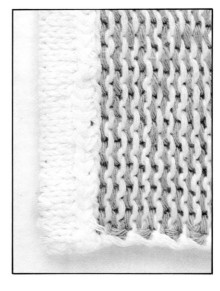

■ BLOCKING AND PRESSING

Before the separate sections of the garment are sewn together, they may have to be blocked into shape so that they match the diagram measurements. This process can be carried out by either pressing with an iron and damp cloth or by dampening the pieces completely.

Place the individual pieces onto a padded surface – an ironing board or a towel or blanket. Pin each piece, right side down, all along the edges so that the rows are horizontal and there is no distortion of the shape. Don't block out or press the ribs or any other raised part of the pattern such as a cable.

For wet blocking, spray the piece with water and leave to dry. For pressing to block, place a damp cloth over the piece of knitting and press each section evenly with a warm iron, pressing down and lifting the iron off the fabric. Do not push the iron over the work as this may distort the fabric.

Whether you have wet the pieces before blocking or they are still damp from the steaming, leave them to dry out naturally.

■ WASHING

The first time a cotton garment is washed, you may notice that the feel of the fabric has altered. There is a tendency for some cotton yarns to bulk up and so feel stiffer. This can also change the overall dimensions. After pressing and wearing, the fabric will relax a little, but not always back to its original tension. For this reason, your tension sample should be washed and retested (see page 110). Wash cotton in lukewarm water with a mild detergent. Do not rub. Rinse several times in lukewarm water and don't wring out to remove excess water. Squeeze or spin for a short time to reduce the bulk of water and consequently the weight. Lay the garment flat on a towel and reshape while damp. Dry away from direct heat.

■ FINISHING TOUCHES

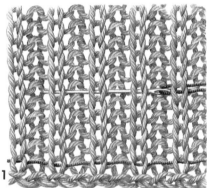

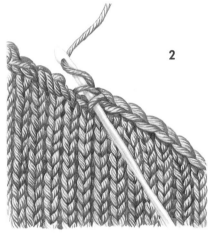

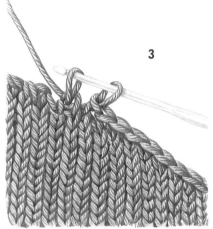

Elastic in ribs (1)
If after the garment is finished you feel the rib is not tight enough, you can thread shirring elastic under the vertical stitches on about every fourth or fifth row of the rib to give a tight even fit. You can knit shirring elastic into the rib at the outset, see page 113.

Taping seams
If you have knitted a large garment in cotton, the weight of the yarn may distort the shape, pulling on the seams so that gradually the shoulder seams will 'grow' in length. To prevent this stretching, sew a narrow ribbon tape along one side of the shoulder seam. Cut the tape to the length of the seam, hold it against the wrong side of one of the shoulder edges and backstitch through the tape and the two pieces of knitting. This will maintain the original length of the shoulder seam and reduce stress on the neckline.

Crochet edge
If the edges of the garment are not ribbed, such as on a waistcoat or a bolero top, it is advisable to neaten and firm up the bottom edge with a trim to prevent it curling. With the right side facing, using a crochet hook approximately the same size as the knitting needles (2), work one row of chain stitch (3) or double crochet. Work the stitches evenly along the edge. It is important that the intervals between the stitches are consistent.

YARN SUPPLIERS

Many of the yarn manufacturers offer a mail-order service. Some companies will send sample yarn cards or lists of stockists on request. Even the major yarn stores in big centres may be able to offer you a mail-order service.

We have chosen to show a length of the main yarn used in the patterns down the side of the first page of the pattern. Should yarns be discontinued or difficult to match, take the book to your local cotton yarn retailer and check their stock against the life-size sample. Your stockist may be able to give you further information and advice about the availability of the yarns. As cotton becomes more popular and more widely used, the availability of the more unusual varieties will improve.

Bobbins
Wesley Hall, Church Street, Whitby, Yorkshire.

Brockwell Wools
Stansfield Mill, Stansfield Mill Lane, Sowerby Bridge, West Yorkshire HX6 3LT.

Creativity
45 New Oxford Street, London WC1.

Colourway
112 Westbourne Grove, London W2.

Designer Yarns
367 Sauchiehall Street, Glasgow G2.

The Handweaver Studio and Gallery Ltd
29 Haroldstone Road, London E17 7AN.

Patons and Baldwins Ltd
Alloa Clackmannanshire, Scotland.

Pamela Wise
Old Loom House, Back Church Lane, London E1.

Phildar (UK) Ltd
4 Gambrel Road, Northampton NN5 5NF.

Pingouin
7-11 Lexington Street, London W1 4BU.

Patricia Roberts
60 Kinnerton Street, London SW1S 8EX.

Ries Wools
242 High Holborn, London WC1.

Rowan Yarns
Green Lane Mill, Holmfirth, West Yorkshire HD7 1RW.

Siop Jen
91 Pontcanna Street, Cardiff, Wales.

Smallwares
17 Galena Road, London W6.

Texere Yarns
Barkerend Road, Bradford, West Yorkshire.

Up Country
Towngate, Holmfirth, West Yorkshire.

The Yarn Store
8 Ganton Street, London W1.

William Hall & Co (Monsall Ltd)
177 Stanley Road, Cheadle Hulme, Cheadle, Cheshire SK8 6RF.

ACKNOWLEDGMENTS

The publishers would like to thank the following people for their help and advice during the production of this book: Julie Dumbrell for pattern writing and checking; Ann Morgan and Sally-Anne Elliott for technical text; Jenny Bancroft for lending her collection of cotton yarn; Vivienne Studholme for knitting samples for photography; Barbara Jones (Artistic Licence) for hair and make-up; Sue Gibson and Rachael Rackow (Bookings) for the modelling; Fanny Rush for the styling for fashion photography; *Accessorize* for all jewellery and sunglasses (except on pages 62, 78, 86); Sheena Salter of the Designers' Collective for introductions to some of the designers; and Mary Tebbs for a final check on the patterns.

Editor Charyn Jones
Art Editor Louise Tucker

Managing Editor Susan Berry
Art Director Debbie MacKinnon

Fashion Photography
Sandra Lousada
Still-life photography
Chris Crofton, assistant Jayne Pearce

Charts and measurement diagrams
David Ashby
Step-by-step illustration
Sandra Pond
Fashion illustration
Sally-Anne Elliott

Reproduction F.E. Burman, London and D.S. Colour International Ltd.

THE DESIGNERS

Vivienne Bannister gave up school teaching to design hand- and machine- knitted garments full time. She sells her designs through retail outlets in London, New York and California and through Partyplan in the southeast of England.
Woodstock, The Avenue, Fairlight, East Sussex.

Sue Bradley is an internationally recognized designer of exciting knitwear. Her patterns are published regularly in magazines and by the yarn companies. A book of her knitwear entitled *Stitches in Time* was published in 1986. Her designs sell in Britain, the United States and Canada.
P.O. Box 549, Bath BA1 1YA.

Joan Chatterley, a graduate of the Royal College of Art, is a busy and prolific designer with her own shop in London. She also sells her designs through retail outlets in the United States and Japan. Her work has been featured in a number of books and magazines, and she designs regularly for a major yarn manufacturer.
40 Moreton Street, London SW1V 2PB.

Lotte Courts is a self-taught knitter. Her interest in knitting started with her training as a painter and her talent for mixing colours. She prefers to work on private commission only.
92 Heath Street, London NW3.

Alison Ellen sells through galleries, exhibitions and on private commission. Most of her designs are knitted in one piece on circular needles and she tries to keep the technique simple while exploring the potential of working with many colours.
Jeffreys Cottage, Dockenfield, Farnham, Surrey.

Sally-Ann Elliott, a graduate of the Royal College of Art in London, specializes in machine-knitted garments for both men and women, and she also designs hand knits and socks. She produces designs for knitwear collections for fashion houses in Britain and Europe. She is a part-time lecturer at the St. Martin's School of Art in London.
669 Wandsworth Road, London SW8.

Toni Hicks and Nadine Hobro are a design partnership who got together to develop a collection of highly original shapes and structures. They have a wide experience of the knitwear industry, having received commissions from home and abroad. They both teach at fashion and textile colleges in London.
3 Holdenby Road, London SE24 2DA.

Zoë Hunt has been associated with Kaffe Fassett for many years. She is now a name in her own right at the top of British knitwear design. She has had her work exhibited and sells her designs by private commission only.
c/o Frances Lincoln Ltd, Apollo Works, 5 Charlton Kings Road, London NW5 2SB.

Ann Morgan worked full time in the fashion industry for some years before deciding to sell her own range of designer knitwear. She currently works as a freelance designer for yarn companies, and produces patterns for brochures as well as one-off designs for magazines. She also works part time as a lecturer in knitwear at the Cheltenham College of Arts and Technology, Gloucestershire.
37A Bathwick Hill, Bath, Avon.

Sue Turton developed her own classic design collection after her long, successful association with Edina Ronay. She now sells throughout Britain and the United States. Her designs are regularly featured in national fashion magazines and she has recently opened a shop in Nottingham selling her own hand knits and designer clothes.
17 Lincoln Grove, Radcliffe on Trent, Nottingham.

Janice Wilkins worked as a designer for a knitting machine manufacturer after graduating from the St. Martin's School of Art. She then set up on her own and now sells both hand knits and machine knits through major retail outlets in Britain, Europe and the United States.
10 Partridge Avenue, Larkfield, Kent ME20 6LT.